THE WHOLESALE DISTRIBUTOR: PURPOSE AND FUNCTIONS

by:

Dr. Don A. Rice
Professor Emeritus
of
Industrial Distribution

A Book for New Employees

THE WHOLESALE DISTRIBUTOR: PURPOSE AND FUNCTIONS

All rights reserved except for use in a review. The reproduction or utilization of this work in any form or by any electronic, mechanical, or other means now known or hereafter invented, including xerography, photo-copying, recording, information storage, or retrieval system, is forbidden without written permission of the publisher.

Copyright 1997

Published by
Darco Press
P.O. Box 5550
Bryan, Texas 77805-5550

Other interesting and informative books by Dr. Rice include:

Financial Transactions of the Wholesale Distributor, a book for newly hired inside and outside salespeople, pricing clerks, counter salespeople, management trainees, and others who deal with markups, discounts, sales, pricing, purchasing, or profits in distribution.

The Guidebook to Service Quality is a "how to implement" text and seminar addressing the implementation of the quality process for distributors. It is intended for those who are interested in increasing their service to customers while lowering their costs and improving their profits and market share.

Dedication

This book is dedicated first to the Lord God Almighty who provides both wisdom and knowledge to those who seek and find His Son, Jesus Christ.

Secondly, it is dedicated to my very good friend and colleague, Dr. Stephen L. Pearce, with whom I am proud to be associated.

Introduction

In order to be a supplier to or a customer of a wholesale distributor you should understand and appreciate the services being provided. The major purpose of this text is to provide information to new distributor employees, university students and new employees of manufacturers who sell through distributors about the advantages of going to market through wholesale distributors.

Serving customers by marketing products through distributors is an exciting and challenging business. Solving customers problems by the application of products purchased through distributors may be the last uncharted frontier in the business world.

In order to chart the course of this multi-billion dollar industry, it will be necessary for both executives and employees to understand where the industry came from and to enjoy the vision of those who see the opportunities for the future. In the past three decades wholesale distributors have proven that they are a viable and cost effective means of marketing products for manufacturers and consumers.

Purpose of This Text

The purpose of this text is to acquaint wholesale distributors, industrial product manufacturer's personnel, their agents, consumers, purchasing managers, buyers, and all others interested in industrial distribution with the importance of the wholesale distributor to both the manufacturers who market products and to the users who consume these products. Every distributor employee and manufacturer's representative or agent should thoroughly understand the services which the wholesale distributor provides for both the manufacturers they represent and the customers they serve. Purchasing managers and buyers should also be knowledgeable about "why manufacturers sell through wholesale distributors" and "why industrial consumers buy from wholesale distributors."

The author has intentionally avoided the inclusion of extensive detail in order to provide the reader with a short, concise explanation of the basic services provided and the requirements of this important segment of the line of distribution.

The chapters on "free enterprise" and "profits" are included to remind readers that the freedom to conduct business in a competitive environment, to strive to be the best, and to conduct business to make a profit, whether providing a product as a manufacturer or a service as a distributor, are the heart and life blood of our great nation. Belief, support and active participation in a free enterprise economy is the only way for people to remain free.

It is particularly important that you, as an employee, (especially a new employee) of a manufacturer or a wholesale distributor, study the information, keeping in mind that this is a growing industry -- an industry whose strength lies in its people. People provide the services wholesale distributors perform for customers. Be assured that you were hired because you were needed, not as a peg to fill a hole in an organization, but as an important part of the employee family. To be productive with a distributor or a manufacturer, you need to understand the purpose and function of the wholesale distributor. The better you understand these functions, the better you can serve your customers and thus be rewarded for your contribution to your company. After you have studied the material, discuss the information with your supervisor so that you become familiar with the philosophy of your company as it pertains to the information presented here.

Table of Contents

Chapter		Page
One	Line of Distribution	1
Two	The Functions Provided by Wholesale Distributors	6
Three	The Functions Performed	14
Four	Economic Advantage, Value Added by Wholesale Distributors	58
Five	Choosing the Marketing Channel	74
Six	The Role of the Manufacturer	86
Seven	Why Contractors and Industrial Users Buy From Wholesale Distributors	102
Eight	Why Manufacturers Market Products Through Wholesale Distributors	120

Chapter		Page
Nine	Investment and Risk	130
Ten	Direct Shipments and Their Profitability	142
Eleven	The Cost of Returned Goods	162
Twelve	Profit and Productivity	180
Thirteen	The Computer as a Distributor Management Tool	202
Fourteen	The Early Years	230
Fifteen	Turn of the Century	238
Sixteen	The Great Depression	248
Seventeen	The War Years	252

ONE

LINE OF DISTRIBUTION

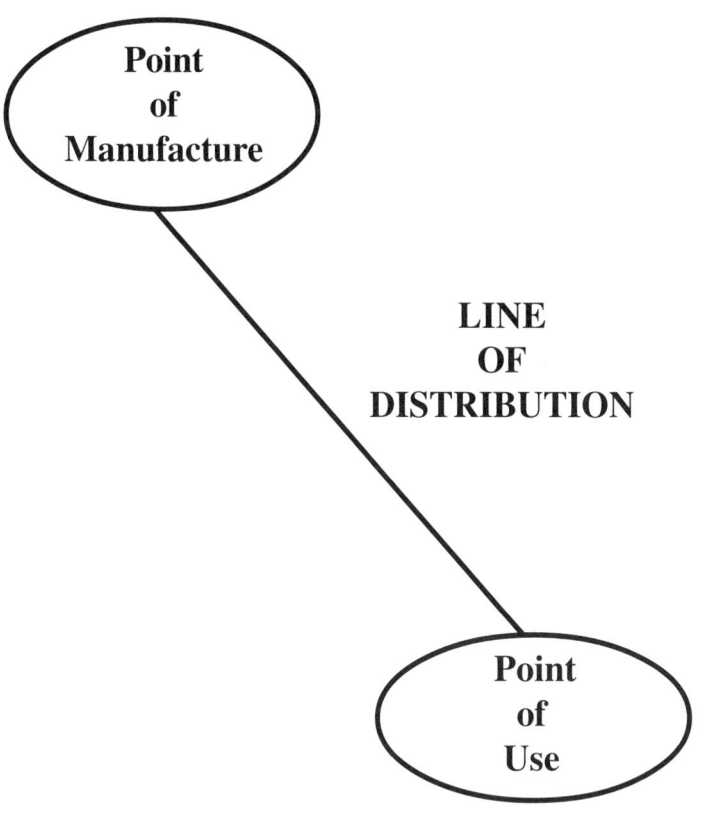

All the movement and physical handling of the materials, paperwork, and payments involved in getting a product from the point of manufacture to the point of use are included in the line of distribution.

The movement of a product from where it is manufactured to where it is to be used is called the line of distribution. Although there are several different channels of distribution from which to choose, there are certain services which must be performed. For example, a customer wants an electronic component. A manufacturer of this product has established a manufacturing plant and a warehouse in Chicago and has the product in inventory. Various electronic distributors have purchased the product and have them in inventory. The customer purchases the component and asks for delivery. The distributor delivers the product for installation and offers service after the sale. The distributor's inventory is replenished from the manufacturer's warehouse. All of these services must be provided regardless of which marketing channel is chosen.

As another example of the line of distribution, an oil field contractor in Odessa, Texas, needs a number of transformers to provide electrical service to oil field pumping equipment. The transformers have been manufactured in New York and shipped to a regional warehouse in Dallas. A local Odessa wholesale distributor has purchased the transformers and has them in inventory for sale to the contractor. Following a sales call by the distributor's outside sales person, the purchasing manager for the contractor calls the distributor and places an order for the transformers. The specifications and requirements are discussed, the proper transformers are identified and picked from inventory, the invoice is cut (written), credit extended, and the transformers are shipped to the contractor's warehouse for later transfer to the point of use, the oil field utility electrical

The economics of how a manufacturer should take products to market must center around the functions required in the marketing sequence.

Five functions must be performed in order to move an industrial product from point of manufacture to point of use. This is true regardless of the marketing channel the manufacturer chooses, assuming a <u>high service level</u> is to be maintained. The person or company which will move the product from the point of manufacturer to the point of use must do the following:

First, the company must maintain a technically qualified sales staff to solve problems of local users of the products to be sold. This includes information concerning the right product for a specific construction project, or engineering information about installation, maintenance or life expectancy, or the design of a complicated automatic control system. The dissemination of this information is part of the service concept. The wholesale distributor salesperson must be technically qualified to assist an architect, contractor, professional purchasing manager or specifying engineer solve whatever problems exist in the design or construction of a plant, a commercial building, a new industrial or electronic product, or maintenance of existing instrumentation or manufacturing equipment.

Second, the company must maintain a local inventory of the merchandise the end user needs and will purchase. Local inventory is essential for most users, particularly for maintenance, repair, and operations items. These are the items needed to build, maintain, repair and/or operate equipment, a manufacturing plant, factory, or mill. When a purchasing manager needs cutting tools, fluids, power transmission equipment, safety equipment or clothing, chemical products or hand tools to use in a manufacturing plant, he expects the distributor to have these materials readily available. For example, when the diaphragm from a pneumatically controlled valve needs replacement, the user wants to purchase the parts locally and usually in a hurry. The availability of these items locally is part of the service the distributor provides for the customer and the manufacturer represented.

Third, the company must extend credit to qualified buyers. Since most orders for industrial goods are placed by telephone, fax, or electronic data interchange (EDI) (as in a request for bids), it is necessary that the supplier (seller) invoice (bill) the buyer for the merchandise purchased. Credit will usually be extended to those industrial companies with a satisfactory record of payment and all which fulfill the requirements of the company credit policy. Those who do not meet the requirements for credit can still be sold merchandise by cash on delivery (COD). The extension of credit is yet another service being provided to the customer by the wholesale distributor.

Fourth, the company must provide transportation of the product from the point of manufacture to the point of use at the buyer's location. Several different methods of transportation are used by companies serving contractors, integrators and industrial customers. Those wholesale distributors who are extremely service-minded may provide delivery by company-owned trucks twice each day, even in large metropolitan areas. Other companies may not own trucks but can ship merchandise by local delivery services. Several companies which specialize in small parts use the United Parcel Service, Federal Express, or other carriers as their delivery system. In any event, the product must be moved from where it was made to where it is stored and eventually to where it is to be used. Transportation which makes products readily available reduces waiting time and is an important service to customers.

Fifth, the company must provide service for the product after the sale. Occasionally a purchased product will not function properly or will not perform as expected. When this happens the purchaser (user) wants immediate response from the supplier (seller) in the form of service. This service could range from providing information about proper operations, redesigning certain aspects of the parts or equipment, or even replacement of faulty merchandise. When this information and assistance is provided by local service people, customer problems should be solved sooner and less expensively.

Example:

A large commercial contractor who built a chemical plant purchased fluid power equipment from a local distributor for fluid process control. During the preliminary testing of the system one of the controllers was discovered to be malfunctioning. The contractor dispatched maintenance to solve the problem. However, the controller was not repairable. The contractor could not continue testing until the controller was changed, and wanted immediate replacement of the item by the supplier. In this case, the local wholesale distributor made another controller available immediately from inventory, which was part of the distributor's service.

A contractor who constructed an office building found that several lighting fixtures were installed which would not work because they contained faulty ballasts. The inspection punch list (things to be corrected) could not be completed until the ballasts were replaced and the lights worked properly. However, because they were purchased from a local distributor who kept ballasts in stock, the contractor could get the replacement parts in a hurry and also depend on the distributor to handle the warranty for him. The distributor provided service after the sale to both the contractor and to the lighting manufacturer.

The wholesale distributor has added value to the product when industrial customers are provided the five services of technically qualified sales personnel, local inventory of goods, extended credit, transportation, and service after the sale.

For more information on these functions, see the units on Functions Performed by the Wholesale Distributor.

SUMMARY

The Five Basic Functions
Involved in Moving a Product
From the Point of Manufacture
To the Point of Use Are:

1. <u>Selling</u>, providing technical information to those who specify, purchase or install electronic or industrial products.

2. Maintaining a local <u>inventory</u> of products on the shelf for immediate delivery.

3. Extending <u>credit</u> to contractors and industrial customers.

4. Providing <u>transportation</u> to the user's location.

5. <u>Servicing</u> products after they have been sold and sometimes even after they have been installed.

13

THREE

THE FUNCTIONS PERFORMED

The functions as outlined earlier in the text will now be discussed in terms of how they are performed, in which department and by whom. The nature of industrial distribution identifies it as a cyclic business. The cycle begins when the distributor buys a product. The product is received and placed in inventory until it is sold. It will then be picked from inventory, packed for shipment, and delivered to the customer. When the customer pays for the merchandise, and has used it satisfactorily, the cycle is completed.

It is often stated in wholesale distribution that "nothing happens until a sale is made." This is true but it should be quickly restated that while selling is vitally important, the sale is not really made (completed) until the money has been collected from the customer and deposited in the bank, and the customer has successfully used the product. At that point, cash is available to repeat the cycle by buying that product or another product for resale to the satisfied customer. Purchasing is the first step in the cycle.

Purchasing

There are two schools of thought concerning the types of products which should be purchased. The first is that the distributor should buy what can be sold. While this sounds logical, it operates under the premise that the distributor will purchase inventory and then send a sales force out to determine to whom it can be sold at a profit. While some wholesalers still operate under this philosophy, most have shifted to a more acceptable method called "customer-based management."

Customer-based management works on the concept that the distributor is in business to serve certain kinds and types of customers. It is the distributor's responsibility to locate the business in reasonable proximity to customers, to understand and serve their purchasing and installation personnel, to determine what they will need and therefore should buy, and to try to provide that product to them at the desired service level and most economical cost.

In either case the distributor will buy in large quantities, boxes or bulk, and will usually sell in smaller quantities or broken packages. This act of buying and breaking down of quantities into smaller lots is a major service that the distributor provides for customers.

Purchasing and Profitability

The purchasing function of the distributorship has the greatest opportunity for profitability within the company. In fact, a two percent decrease in the cost of goods, which the distributor gets and keeps (does not allow the outside sales force to pass on to the customer through lower prices) will make the same contribution to pre-tax profits as a 50 percent increase in sales if the distributor makes three percent net profit before tax. Which do you suppose would be the easier to obtain, a two percent decrease in the cost of goods or a 50 percent increase in sales? When the net profit before tax is lower, say two percent or one and one-half percent, the two percent saving on the cost of goods would be equal to 75 percent or 100 percent increase in sales, respectively.

A two percent reduction in the cost of goods can be achieved by several methods, including buying in large quantities, purchasing before a price increase, buying sufficient quantities to get a freight allowance equal to two percent of the product cost, taking the cash discounts which manufacturers provide to the distributor, buying special promotional items which carry larger discounts, conducting a sufficient volume of business with a manufacturer over an extended period of time so that a "factory rebate" of two percent or more is earned or getting the manufacturer to participate in a local advertising campaign for the product which is equal to a two percent discount on the product.

Because of the high profit impact potential in purchasing, it is one of the most important professional staff responsibilities in the wholesale distributorship. More money can be made here more easily than in any other segment of the business.

Even though this is true, many distributor managers fail to see the connection between highly trained purchasing people and greater profits.

One of the primary reasons is that there is no generally accepted reward system which financially recognizes purchasing managers and buyers for obtaining the best quality products at the lowest possible cost (not price). Some advances, however, are being made and today more purchasing managers are being rewarded on their contribution to gross margin much the same as outside salespeople. Also, there is training and certification available through the National Association of Purchasing Managers in Tempe, Arizona, which can result in one's becoming a certified purchasing manager.

Another serious problem which exists between sales and purchasing is that invariably, when the purchasing people are successful in getting a significant saving in the cost of the product, management allows outside sales personnel to pass this saving through to the customer, even though keeping it would mean a significant increase in pre-tax profitability. There are times, of course, when at least a portion of that saving must be passed on to customers in order to be competitive. However, very little market research is actually done by most distributor management to ascertain exactly what prices the market will bear so they can consistently try to sell at the highest price. All too many take the easy way out and try to get the order with the lowest price even though the sale may provide little or no profit.

Price and, consequently, profit are also affected by product line acceptability. If the distributorship is well established, it probably possesses some of the more widely accepted product lines which are customarily used by manufacturers, contractors, engineering firms, electronic technicians, and industrial plants. These product lines would include, but not be limited to, fluid power equipment, fasteners, welding supplies, chemicals, power transmission equipment, cutting tools and fluids, safety supplies and equipment, sanitary supplies, electrical machinery and supplies, materials handling equipment, electronic components, industrial rubber goods, textile supplies, oil field equipment and hand tools.

When an item or items from the product line are in short supply in the distributor's warehouse, the purchasing manager checks the order-point-order-quantity formulas which indicate when and how many to purchase. After this, the purchase order is faxed to the manufacturer to replenish the warehouse stock.

A better method is to send the order by electronic order entry. This method is known as Electronic Data Interchange (EDI). When using electronic order entry the distributor places the purchase order directly with the manufacturer from one computer directly to another. There are many advantages in this method. It shortens the length of time to place an order in the hands of the manufacturer and does not rely upon the inconsistencies of the United States Postal Service. There is also less opportunity for errors since the transmission is direct and from one computer to another. Reasonably accurate order entry clerks, when entering an order received by fax or voice, will average one error in every 250 keystrokes, but the computer only one in five million. After the order has been placed with the manufacturer, the distributor waits for the product to be delivered to the receiving dock.

Receiving the Product

It is very important to the accountability of the distributor operation that the material which was ordered be received in a timely and accurate manner. An error created at this point leads to errors later on in the identification of the goods and the quantity received, and literally affects the entire distributor operation, including purchasing, inventory, sales, payables and warehousing.

Most often, merchandise arrives at the wholesale distributors receiving dock by truck. Once it is unloaded into the warehouse the bill of lading should be carefully checked to see that the number of cartons specified is exactly the same as the number of cartons received. Each address label should be checked to see that the packages received were in fact those shipped to this company. When these things have been checked, the driver will request that the bill of lading be signed, showing proof of delivery.

Lighter shipments and rush shipments often arrive by parcel post, United Parcel Service (UPS), or by one of several express (overnight delivery) carriers. On occasion, the distributor's company vehicles will bring material to the receiving department when it has been "bought out" from competitors to fill rush orders for the customer or when materials have been transferred from another company branch.

It is commonly accepted practice in many wholesale distributorships to have trainees and other new employees working in the receiving department. While it is true that new employees must start in the warehouse in order to learn the products, paper flow and general business operations, it is the contention of the author that the receiving area is of such a critical nature that new employees should not start there, but in fact should start with picking, packing, and shipping instead of receiving.

The rationale is that when orders are being picked and packed for shipment management will have at least one and sometimes as many as three check points between the picking and the shipping to catch any errors which have been made. In contrast, in receiving there are generally no such checks. If the material is labeled incorrectly, entered incorrectly, or stored in the wrong place in the warehouse, it may be months before these errors are detected and corrected.

After trainees have been thoroughly indoctrinated and have some experience picking and packing, they are much better qualified to work in receiving. They will know what products are being received, be able to properly identify them and place them on the shelves in the proper location. They will also be familiar with the paperwork and be able to expedite receiving judiciously.

After the products and paperwork have been properly documented, they can be moved to a receiving area for unpacking. This needs to be a secure and protected area to guarantee that materials are not removed prematurely to fill invoices for customers before the receiving process is completed and to ensure that theft does not take place.

Inside the secure area, the products are unpacked and examined carefully to determine that breakage has not occurred. Bar coding labels can then be attached, assuming that it was not done by the manufacturer.

Before the materials are moved from the secure area, it is very important that they be checked against the distributor's purchase order to see that what was ordered was in fact what was shipped and received. The distributor's purchase order must be verified by the manufacturer's packing slip and double-checked against the materials actually received. The goods should be checked carefully as to their identity, the quantity by actual count, and the quality required. This last step needs to be completed carefully to ensure that the goods were not damaged in shipment. Any concealed damage, not readily discernable when the freight bill was signed, should now be reported to the carrier.

There are several methods used for final checking of the merchandise received. They vary in thoroughness and expense. The most complete and thorough check is called the blind check which is made without the availability of an invoice. In this case the cartons are opened and the content of each package is recorded by actual count. When every item has been counted, checked for proper quality, and recorded, this record is sent to the purchasing department for comparison with the invoice which was received from the factory. The invoice is also checked against the purchase order to ensure that the goods received were what were ordered. If the shipment is acceptable and the count is accurate, then the materials can be released to be put on the shelf as inventory for resale.

While this is a very accurate method, it is very time-consuming and expensive. A more satisfactory check is called the invoice check.

The manufacturer, upon receipt of the distributor's order, prints the invoice, sends notice to the warehouse for filling and mails the invoice to the distributor. The invoice is compared by the distributor against the original purchase order to see that they are the same. The information is then sent to the receiving department for checking against the packing slip attached to one of the cartons. The packing slip indicates the type and number of items shipped. Once it has been determined by receiving that the information is correct, the packing slip and other documentation are forwarded to the accounting department for payment and the materials are released to the warehouse for placement on the shelf. This is a somewhat faster yet less reliable method than the blind check.

Bar Code Scanning

Bar code scanning is the fastest, most reliable and most accurate method of receiving merchandise. When manufacturers have pre-fixed bar code scanning labels on their cartons and when the distributor's method of identifying those products are the same, a hand-held wand can be scanned across the labels to rapidly identify the product and the number enclosed. This can be transmitted directly to the distributor's computer via several methods and can automatically be cross-checked with the purchase order submitted. Exceptions can be printed out in the purchasing department. If the amount purchased was in fact the amount received, the material can be released immediately to the warehouse for storage.

Regardless of the receiving method, it is vital that, upon acceptance, the paperwork be correct and the products be moved quickly to the warehouse for storage. This gives immediate access to the salespeople who may have orders waiting for the merchandise.

Products are usually ordered in full cartons or quantities called standard packages. It is advantageous to the distributor to sell them in the same full carton lots. In fact, customers are encouraged to buy larger quantities and price breaks are often given to those who will buy in standard packages. Therefore, sealed cartons should be placed on the shelf in an orderly fashion. The sealed containers also reduce the risk of breakage or loss to theft during storage.

In most cases there will still be merchandise on the shelf when the new shipment arrives. This occurs because distributors try to provide approximately a 95 percent fill rate (orders filled from stock) for their customers on the most widely sold items (commonly called the "A" items). This means that 95 percent of the time when new merchandise is received one or more items will still be on the shelf. Only five percent of the time should the distributor be "out-of-stock" on an "A" item when the new merchandise arrives. Therefore, it is important that existing stock be rotated to the front of the shelf in order to accomplish first-in-first-out inventory handling which assures the customer of obtaining fresh merchandise.

In many distributorships, there will not be sufficient space on the shelf if existing products are there when the new shipment arrives. This means that extra storage somewhere else in the warehouse must be provided and that the material must be stored there until it can be moved to its usual storage location when needed for filling immediate orders. This will create many problems if the products are stored where they cannot be found at the time they are needed. However, computerization of the storage process and bin locations can be very helpful. When materials are stored in locations other than their standard place, the computer can remember the location and lead the searcher to the materials for immediate retrieval. Computerization at this point offers a very decided advantage for the distributor with this capability.

Warehouse Storage

Once the receiving process has been completed, the merchandise is moved into the warehouse storage area. These products make up the physical inventory from which customer orders are filled. This is the largest single financial investment made by the distributor owners. In fact, 80 to 90 percent of the distributor's investment will be in inventory (items on the shelf) and receivables (those materials which have been sold but have not been paid for by the customer). The inventory is usually the largest investment of the two because sufficient inventory will be kept in-stock to cover approximately two to three months of total sales. By comparison, if customers paid their bills in 45 days, on the average, then the investment in receivables would constitute approximately 38.5 percent of the total value of the money invested in inventory and receivables.

Example of Goods Sold From Stock:

Annual Sales	$5,000,000
Annual Cost of Goods Sold	$4,000,000
Average Inventory	$1,000,000

Average Accounts Receivable = $\frac{\$5,000,000}{360 \text{ days}} \times 45 \text{ days} = \$625,000$

Average Inventory Investment	$1,000,000
Plus Average Accounts Receivable	$ 625,000
Average Investment	$1,625,000

For example, if a distributor sold $5 million of product out of warehouse stock in a year, and if the materials cost $4 million when purchased, the average distributor would keep about $1 million worth of inventory in the warehouse.

This investment would be in addition to the money customers owed for the merchandise purchased on credit but not paid for, which might average 45 days worth of sales. In this case it would be about $625,000 to make the total investment $1,625,000.00.

Since 80 percent of these sales will be from "A" items, it is the responsibility of the purchasing department to determine the proper mix of merchandise in the warehouse. As discussed earlier, "A" items constitute 80 percent of the distributor's sales but represent only 20 percent of the line items in the warehouse.

In arranging the storage bins for the merchandise it is important to have "A" items strategically placed. Warehouse floor layouts vary widely from distributor to distributor but are generally arranged by manufacturer's product with fast moving items being closer to the counter for easy access by counter salespeople.

The distributor owner, because of the large investment and high inventory carrying cost, wants to keep the inventory as low as possible while maintaining the highest possible order fill rate (service level) from that inventory. The cost to own inventory is 20 percent plus the cost of money. This means that if interest on borrowed money was 10 percent, then the annual inventory carrying cost would be 20 percent plus the 10 percent cost of money which would total 30 percent of the inventory. For example $100,000 in inventory would cost the distributor $30,000 to own for one year.

Another consideration which affects the storage areas in which the merchandise is located is protection against loss or theft. Any theft or loss by damage of material in the warehouse or during shipment from the distributor to the customer is very expensive indeed. Few employees actually realize the cost incurred. Suppose, for example, a worker damages $170 worth of grinding wheels by accidentally dropping the carton too hard on the floor. Most employees would consider this to be a $170 loss. While this is true, in actuality the loss is much greater because of the cost to purchase and carry the inventory up to the point of damage.

Even more devastating is the fact that the only way for the distributor to make up that loss is to sell sufficient dollars of items to recover the $170 in net profit before tax. If the distributor is an average distributor and makes two percent net profit before tax, $8,500 worth of merchandise must be sold in order to recover the $170 cost of the grinding wheels ($170 divided by two percent [.02] = $8,500.00).

If we assume that the inventory had a 30 percent inventory carrying cost, you must multiply the $170 by 1.30 and then divide by two percent which indicates that $11,050 worth of merchandise has to be sold for the distributor to break even on the damage of $170. The distributor has handled all this merchandise and still not made a profit. Since profit is the only means of job security, it behooves every warehouse person to ensure that materials held there are neither damaged nor stolen. This is every employee's responsibility.

While most employees of the wholesale distributorship are perfectly honest and would never steal from their employer, occasionally some unscrupulous person will be hired unbeknownst to the management. It is the responsibility of the honest employees to help keep warehouse materials under surveillance and ensure their availability for sale to the customer and therefore, a reasonable profit to the employer.

Because this is so important, management many times feels it necessary to provide other security measures such as electronic surveillance, TV cameras and monitors. In many cases it has also resorted to polygraph equipment tests.

One of the quickest ways to reduce theft of merchandise is to limit the number of entrances and exits to and from the warehouse and provide security at these points. Lighting secure areas is also a factor. Proper lighting has always been a deterrent to those who would break in and steal merchandise. Properly lighted areas also provide less opportunity for accidents and greater operating efficiency.

Having a perpetual inventory count is also helpful in securing the merchandise and helps the distributor quickly recognize areas where merchandise is not properly secured and may be found missing.

The ultimate inventory control is executed when all items that leave the warehouse are listed on a shipping ticket, with no exceptions.

Sales

Now that the merchandise has been purchased, received, properly checked and placed on the shelf, and the inventory records have been updated, it is now ready for sale to contractors or industrial customers. There are three methods of selling this merchandise which will be discussed briefly. They are counter sales, inside telephone sales, and outside sales. All of these are professional selling positions and should be considered as such.

Professional selling is considered problem-solving selling and is unlike personal selling associated with retail selling to the general public. In professional selling, the customer is more concerned with the quality, the products performance, and getting questions answered regarding availability, maintenance requirements, the accessibility of repair parts, product recycling, and service after the sale. Problem-solving selling also deals with interchangeability of existing products and substitute products, should there be a need.

In order to fulfill the requirements of professional selling, the person needs to be highly trained, possess professional selling techniques, have a pleasant personality and helpful attitude, enjoy helping other people solve their product problems, and be willing to develop a good working relationship with customers. Only this combination will result in professional problem-solving selling.

The Counter Salesperson

Many wholesale distributorships, for the convenience of their local customers, offer a city counter as well as a "will-call" area. Both may be located within the same warehouse area but each should be used differently.

The city counter usually consists of a product display area and a counter which separates the customer from the inventory storage area. The counter salesperson waits on the customer, fills the order, and writes an invoice for the material at the time of purchase. The salesperson also answers questions concerning the technical aspects of the product, its installation, and proper usage. The counter person may also be responsible for technical adaptation of products, i.e., determining the correct holding coil for a motor starter or the correct overload protection ("heaters") for that starter under the circumstances predetermined by the size of the motor to be controlled. This requires a great deal of knowledge about the product, its application, current ratings and eventual usage.

It is very important that the counter salespeople develop the charisma discussed earlier because they are in direct contact with the customer on a face-to-face basis. They must also merchandise, promote and organize product promotions and displays. They must look the part, act the part, and in fact be the professional people required. To the customer, these individuals represent the entire company at that point in time.

Using the "will-call" facility is different from utilizing the city sales counter but has an added advantage. The customer can still come by the wholesale distributorship and pick up products, having quick, ready access to the material, and it is available without waiting for the order to be filled. The will-call area is a place to store, for ready access, those materials which the customer previously ordered by phone, fax, or EDI. This prevents the customer from waiting while the order is being filled and the invoice prepared.

Because of the immediate proximity of the counter and will-call area to the warehouse, the counter sales and will-call personnel in some businesses report to the warehouse supervisor even though they fulfill a sales function. This is not true of the inside salespeople who usually report directly to the sales manager.

Inside Sales

It is quite common for the inside salesperson to have served on the city counter prior to assignment to the inside sales or telephone staff. At the counter, the person receives good product knowledge, learns to respond to customer questions and relate to merchandise on the shelf. However, in the inside sales role the person will not be dealing with customers face-to-face, but will be taking their telephone calls for merchandise and problem solving.

This type of sales is much more difficult because the salesperson does not have actual parts to see, facial expressions to follow, nor hand signals and body language to read when responding to the customer. A typical telephone conversation for a wholesale distributor inside salesperson might go something like this. The customer says, "I have a part that is black, is round on the outside, has a square hole in the middle, and has two wires sticking out of it, and I need one." The steady inside salesperson says, "We sure would like to sell you one — what do you think it is?" The customer replies, "I don't know what they call it." The distributor salesperson says, "Where did you get it?" Customer's response, "It came out of a motor starter." Being knowledgeable and understanding that the customer has just described a holding coil, the inside salesperson leads the customer through the proper steps to identify the make, style, size, and voltage in order to sell the customer the proper item.

The inside salesperson must be continually aware that this is professional and problem-solving selling. The customer has some piece of machinery which is not operational because it needs this holding coil. It is a problem for the customer and an opportunity for the company. If the salesperson solves the problem quickly and appropriately, it will make the distributor look good in the eyes of the customer. If machinery is down and needs to be made operational quickly, this is probably a will-call item. The customer will dispatch a driver to pick up the repair part or ask the distributor to send out a "hot shot" (rapid delivery service) so that the part can be installed and operations can resume immediately.

Not all of the items that will be requested of the inside salesperson will be demanded on an emergency basis. In fact, not all of the materials will be in-stock. A certain percentage, three to ten percent for electronic or industrial houses and up to 50 percent for some contractor houses, will be "special order" or drop-shipped items. This means that the inside salesperson must be completely familiar with the manufacturer's terms of sale, minimum order size, lead times, freight rates, and cancellation charges for work in progress, to name a few.

In order to determine these things, the inside salesperson will have a number of electronic catalogs or electronic data bases readily available. Since each manufacturer's terms and conditions of sale are likely to be different, the salesperson must check the references carefully before placing the order.

The inside sales area is an exciting place to work. It is literally the heartbeat of the distributorship. If the distributorship is conducting business as it should, the telephones will be continually ringing and the pressure will be on the inside salesperson to respond quickly to customer demands. Sometimes customers know exactly what they want and give you the make, model and even the numbers from your own catalog. More often, however, customers are trying to solve a problem for which they need a product, but do not know the distributor part number. In addition, they want to know whether or not the product will fulfill their needs. If it will, they want to know the price and whether or not the product is available. To be successful, the inside salesperson must be a complete product information person who can communicate facts and ideas to customers by phone.

Once it has been determined what the customer needs, a purchase order number is requested from the buyer and the order is entered into the computer, or written by hand depending upon the capabilities of the distributorship.

Because product knowledge is so vital to the success of the inside salesperson, all will be required to attend product training sessions conducted by manufacturers at the distributor's location as well as attend some factory schools which provide product information for distributor's personnel. In these training sessions, manufacturers will be informing the salespeople of the features and benefits of their product and should also stress how their products can best be sold against the competition.

Inside salespeople in some companies have the ability to make price determinations, within certain guidelines, at the time of the sale. It is important that they understand that it is never the intent of the well-managed distributor to sell strictly on price. In fact, the profitable distributor will be a little high, but will be worth it in the eyes of the customer. Worth to the customer can usually be tied to service level provided. The service level is enhanced when the customer is given cost saving, problem solving information, the product is on the shelf and is readily available to the customer.

Price and product availability go hand in hand. When there is a question about availability, it is sometimes necessary for the inside salesperson to run to the warehouse and check stock (see that the product is actually on the shelf). However, if the proper inventory management procedures have been implemented, and cycle counting has been done properly and recorded on a computerized system, the computer will have the correct information and will save the time the inside salesperson would need to go to the warehouse and actually check the amount of merchandise on the shelf.

Correct computerized inventory knowledge is time saving for the customer as well as the distributor. It is also the most cost efficient method. The speed at which the inside salesperson serves the customer is important, but accuracy in providing the customer exactly what is wanted to solve the problem is even more important. Therefore, excellent and accurate communication is essential. Inside salespeople should take sufficient time to question the customer thoroughly so that they know and deliver exactly what the customer wants and needs.

In most companies, the inside sales position is a rewarding job and some people make their career there. Others use it as a step in the career path to outside sales and eventually to sales management.

Outside Sales

Outside salespeople must have all the attributes of the inside salesperson plus many additional characteristics. First and foremost they must look and conduct themselves as professionals, building satisfactory personal relationships with customers to endear themselves in the minds of those they serve. Since the outside salesperson meets customers personally, the relationship is usually enhanced by friendly and casual business relationships. The outside salesperson must in fact be a specialist in the customer's business, having sufficient product knowledge to advise customers of goods and services which will fill their product needs, save them money by reducing their operating costs, and thus solve their problems.

While some outside salespeople do take orders for products from customers, most are salespeople who advise customers and help them solve their problems. Then they refer the customers to the inside salespeople at the wholesale distributorship for the actual purchase.

Some distributors have inside and outside salespeople who are responsible for the same customer base which facilitates the customer getting to know both the outside salesperson and the inside salesperson on a personal basis making the customer feel more comfortable. Other companies refer calls from customers to any inside salesperson available at the time. Either method can work well when administered properly.

Most outside salespeople tend to be college graduates, or be somewhat older, and in the case of wholesale distributors, have tremendous product knowledge. In addition, it is very helpful for them to be excellent listeners. Listening with perception is difficult, but important to the salesperson who is trying to identify problems or special needs in order to better serve the customer.

    Unlike the inside salesperson who will be responsible for generating the paperwork and seeing the order through to its completion, the outside salesperson may not deal directly with the product at all during the order filling and completion process but will work strictly with the customer. Because of this relationship, it is important that the outside salesperson be completely informed as to the status of the customer's orders, particularly with backorders, orders completed and orders awaiting shipment, to be able to discuss these intelligently with the customer on the next sales call.

    While the outside salesperson's primary responsibility may be calling on purchasing managers, buyers, contractors, or industrial customers, it is also customary for this person to call on architects and specifying engineers. This is especially true when new energy saving products like heating and air conditioning equipment, specialty lighting and similar items are introduced to the market and would be appropriate for a new building being designed.

Sales Manager

The sales manager is responsible for the training, coordination, evaluation, and technical expertise of both the inside and outside sales force. The salespeople operate directly under the supervision and are responsible to the manager for their sales activities. It is the manager's primary responsibility to set sales goals and quotas for salespeople, help identify the important accounts and primary products to be sold to those accounts, to evaluate the results and reward those who meet the desired objectives.

The career path for most sales managers is through the warehouse, to counter sales, then to inside sales. When they have developed an extremely fine record as an outside salesperson, they may be considered for promotion to sales manager.

The sales manager also has a major role in determining what product lines to take on (purchase) and inventory. This requires that this person have sufficient knowledge of the customer base to determine what products the customer should need and will buy. These decisions are usually made in conjunction with the salespeople who have the responsibility of selling the product to the customer.

The sales manager in a small company will report directly to the president, while in a larger company, report to a vice president of sales.

Another very important aspect of the wholesale distributor is the quotations department. This is also a fertile training ground for many would-be distributor managers.

Contractor customers are constantly seeking opportunities to submit bids for mass residential, commercial and industrial projects. When a series of apartment complexes, major chemical plant, steel mill, automobile assembly plant or other manufacturing facility is to be bid, the general contractors usually contact several sub-contractors and provide them with blueprints and programs of requirements which they break down into bills of material for the purpose of submitting a bid for labor and materials. In such a case, the mechanical contractor would choose one or more pipe-valve-and-fitting (PVF) distributors and request that they submit bids for the bill of materials to be installed on the job if the bid is successful. Because the construction industry is very competitive, the contractor is very price sensitive both on the bill of materials and on the labor requirements, knowing that the low bidder will most likely get the opportunity to build the plant. Therefore, a great deal of pressure is put on the distributor to provide the best product at the lowest possible cost. If the sub-contractors (electrical, mechanical, plumbing, structural) provide the most competitive bids to the general contractor, this enhances the general contractor's chances of success in securing the bid. If the general contractor gets the job, the successful sub-contractor and the associated PVF distributor will get the order for the materials quoted. This is a domino effect for unsuccessful bidders, but is very much a part of selling and providing service to the construction industry.

Therefore, two major questions arise. One deals with price, the other with availability.

In the final analysis, the price is determined by a perceived value in the mind's eye of the eventual consumer. For example, one potential customer may see materials handling equipment simply as a means of doing something people cannot do and is therefore willing to settle for the least expensive equipment available. Another potential buyer may believe that properly-sized and well-manufactured materials handling equipment not only saves time and money, thus improving the efficiency of the work force, but is also a significant safety factor, which also reduces costs. The more we know about what the customer needs and wants and the closer the specifications can be written the easier it is for the distributor to determine what the bid should contain.

Oftentimes, very large customers, such as automobile manufacturers, will require that extra pricing concessions be made by the distributor's manufacturer in order for the distributor to supply the products or services. With major customers of this type, the buyers may request that the product be "drop shipped" directly to the plant and never enter the distributor's inventory. This reduces the cost of shipping and handling and these savings can be passed on to the customer in the form of a lower product price.

Lower prices do not necessarily connote lower costs. The author remembers a particular job for which the contractor bid the lighting to be drop shipped directly to the commercial building under renovation. As it happened, the lighting equipment, usually installed near the end of the job, arrived the third week into a nine-month renovation project. During the remaining time the fixtures had to be physically moved from floor to floor in order to be out of the way of the construction workers. This physical handling cost many dollars. Also during the move, many lighting fixtures were broken and some stolen. The question therefore arises: Which was the most important — the price or the cost?

Because there is always pressure to sell for less, the quotations department must have rigorous guidelines set by the distributor management which establish the lowest margins to use when calculating selling price on various materials in inventory. Because of the expense involved, there is always business which the distributor cannot afford to take. In this light it is critical for the quotations department to know what services will be demanded of the distributor by the customer once the order has been placed. If the service demands are high, then sufficient margin must be built into the price to fulfill the service requirements. Every invoice cut and every delivery to the customer costs the distributor money. If these were not calculated into the quoted price, then the services provided to the customer are conducted at a loss.

Another aspect of the quotations department when determining price is to "leave nothing on the table." There are three pricing schemes available to distributors, two of which leave nothing on the table (quoting the lowest price by a considerable margin leaves profit on the table). The first is to be higher than the competition, but be fully worth the higher charge by providing additional service which the customer wants and is willing to pay for. The second would be to meet the price of the competition and provide exactly the same product at exactly the same price but with slightly better service in order to get the order. The third scheme is to have the lowest price and therefore, secure the order on price alone. The latter seems to be the business practice preferred by many distributors. This is not a solution to which the author subscribes because any time you sell a product cheaper than someone else, you in fact walked away from available profit (you left it on the table). If the quotations management is predisposed to sell lower, then at least sell only one-half of a percent or less below the competition, not two percent. Try not to leave anything on the table.

It should be pointed out that customers should be buying on "quality" not on price. Quality is defined as "meeting the customer requirements" -- no more, no less. Buying on quality means that the customer is serious about the "total cost" not the initial price of products or services. It does very little good to have a low price on a product which costs the customer more money in the long run. For example, the customer may purchase a grinding wheel for a lower price from one distributor than from another. But price should not be the sole consideration. The cheaper wheel may take twice the time to put the finish on the part or it may not grind to the proper surface criteria. The wheel may have been cheaper, but the process much more expensive. Another consideration in the pricing scheme is availability. A distributor will sometimes offer a low price, but not have the product in stock for immediate delivery. Materials which cannot be delivered in a timely fashion can be very expensive to the customer in lost machining time and lost labor.

It is customary in many industries for purchasing managers, who are not in the quality process, to put out a call for bids on supplies or equipment. The author believes that when bids are tendered, they should seldom, if ever be mailed, but should be hand carried to the customer by the outside salesperson. The salesperson should explain the bid to the purchasing manager and specifically thank the customer for past business and "ask for the order." If you do not ask for the order you probably will not get it. The distributorship will be much more successful when quotation personnel and outside salespeople work together to serve the customer and get the order.

People making quotes should also be aware of the carry-through involved in serving the customer. If the distributor was successful in securing the order, then the job was not finished but only started when the quotation was delivered. Let us assume for the purposes of discussion that a manufacturing facility is being readied to manufacturer a new product and that new consumable supplies (those consumed in the manufacturing process) have been awarded to a local wholesale distributor by virtue of a successful bid. Let's assume that the distributor had bid the materials out of warehouse stock. The customer now needs the first bill of materials to be delivered in order to start the manufacturing process. The second round of activity in the distributorship begins when the customer prepares this purchase order.

This order may come to the distributor via the telephone, through computer to computer transmission as in EDI, or by fax. If the order is delivered orally, it will generally be accepted by the inside salesperson who will enter it into the computer for transmission to the order processing department. Via the fax, the order will go directly to the order processing department where it will be entered into the computer.

When the order is received, the credit worthiness of the customer is checked to determine whether credit can be extended or whether the material must be shipped cash on delivery (C.O.D.). When the credit worthiness of the customer has been approved, the purchase order goes immediately to pricing. With a bid, the pricing ordinarily is checked against the bid and entered in the computer. Matching the pricing with the bid can be a complicated process and many errors could occur.

The pricing people must take into consideration any additional discounts earned or taken, additional pricing structures provided by the manufacturer for a special order, cash discounts, terms of payment and any other special pricing arrangements made with the customer.

Pricing of industrial products fluctuates widely for several reasons. The foremost is caused by the volatility of the price of raw materials such as copper, silver, steel and petroleum-based products. In addition, supply, demand and availability, often dictated by market conditions, also affect pricing. Price fluctuations necessitate continual checking of prices to make sure that the price quoted is one which provides the distributor with the highest possible margin available in the current market. This is the responsibility of the sales manager and the pricing clerk. Keep in mind that the salesperson always seems to want the lowest price to make it easier to get the order. This is seldom in the best interest of the distributor. Therefore, pricing is a continual opportunity for the well-informed distributor to increase profits.

Even after all the products are priced and extended (price per each multiplied by the number purchased), this may or may not be the eventual price which the customer pays.

Variations in the amount paid may be caused by cash discounts extended or other adjustments which may be made for handling, transportation, mis-shipments, returns, or local taxes. The amount paid may, in some cases, even be lower than the invoice amount.

Order Filling

Now that the price has been calculated and credit has been checked and approved, the order is ready to be filled. A common term for order filling is called picking, which is followed by packing and shipping. These units, commonly known as "picking, packing and shipping," will be discussed separately.

Order filling is one of the most important jobs in the wholesale distributorship. You can have the finest purchasing manager, inside salesperson, quotations, pricing personnel, operations people, and outside salesperson, and all of them may have completed their jobs precisely, but if the order picker chooses the wrong product, or fails to find something on the shelf which the customer needs, then the customer is not satisfied and may choose another distributorship from which to buy next time. Therefore, it is very important that the picker know exactly where merchandise is located both on the shelf and in reserve and that the person be able to fill the order in a correct and timely manner.

Order filling sequences vary from distributor to distributor but basically all of the orders to be filled will go to one person for distribution to the pickers. Before giving clearance for picking, this person usually will review the orders to determine that they have been properly processed and approved for picking. They should have been "logged in" by the computer and assigned a processing number along with an invoice number.

In some systems, picking routes and package labels will have been pre-printed by the computer. The computer also has pre-determined the most efficient route the picker will take through the warehouse. The pre-printed labels are attached to the packing boxes as the products are readied for shipment.

Depending upon the size and quantity of the material to be picked, different handling methods may be utilized. In some cases, forklifts or electric pallet movers will be used for large orders or heavy merchandise. Where the products are smaller and the space more confined, small carts or baskets may be used. Some are stored in carrousels which move the merchandise to the picker instead of the picker going to the merchandise. This method is widely used in the electronics distribution industry.

In other mechanized systems, conveyors will be used to move the material from the place where it is picked to the staging or packing area. Where space and inventory shrinkage (theft) are problems, stacker cranes are often used which stack inventory from one to several stories high in warehouse storage bins. A small electrified cart which will move either vertically or horizontally is employed in a one-man operation which takes the picker (cart operator) directly to the bin containing the necessary merchandise for picking. In confined areas this is an excellent method of conveyance, but may be more expensive.

In the other sophisticated systems, computerized order picking is also available. A common method is the use of a computerized robot to retrieve trays, baskets or bins which contain the product needed. The customers order is placed in the computer which determines the picking order. The computer then directs the robot to retrieve the trays which are brought to floor level where the order picker removes the material. The computer tells the robot to put the tray back in its original location or another location and to remember where it is located. It is not uncommon for computerized materials handling buildings to be 70 or more feet tall and contain thousands of trays in which to store merchandise.

Regardless of the method, it is usually necessary for the picker to fill more than one order at a time, thus reducing high labor costs. An individual who can fill two, three or more orders at one time can thus reduce the labor costs for the distributor significantly.

It is the responsibility of the pickers to be extremely accurate in choosing the items which are on the purchase order.

Even when they are, occasionally an error will be made by choosing the wrong product or the wrong quantity. Thus, most distributors provide checkers to ensure that the order is filled properly. The implementation of the quality process is the most significant thing the distributor can do to cut the cost of errors in the picking process. The widely accepted inspection method does not find all of the errors and it adds to the cost of the picking process.

The customer places an order with the distributor when a need arises for the material or service. It is very disconcerting to the customer when the order arrives late at the plant or construction site, it is either the wrong product or the wrong amount, or is billed incorrectly. To keep errors to an absolute minimum, checkers work diligently to compare the purchase order with the pick ticket. They then check the material which the picker has "pulled" (material taken from the shelf) against the invoice to ensure that the materials are delivered as requested.

Because customers are demanding greater accuracy from distributors, some companies have two, three or even more checkers. Sometimes a supervisory person performs this function. This is very expensive indeed. This cost may be justified where young or inexperienced pickers are working and learning in pressure situations, but steps must be taken to see that pickers are properly trained, have the proper system and are motivated to do the job properly. Excellent service at the lowest cost can only be obtained when pickers make no (zero) errors, without being checked.

Customers expect quality service which literally translates into "zero defects." This means that the distributor must deliver all of the products in the right quality, the right quantity, in the right amount and bill the customer correctly 100 percent of the time. Through research conducted by the faculty of the Thomas A. Read Center for Distribution Research and Education at Texas A&M University it was learned that when orders were filled with the wrong merchandise, and the item was returned by the customer, not only did the distributor lose the confidence of the customer, but both the distributor and customer suffered considerable financial loss.

The return involves paperwork and material handling which includes picking up the merchandise from the customer, inspecting for damage, and physically placing it back on the shelf. Additional paperwork is also necessary to return the item, including sending the paperwork to the shipping or transportation department, issuing the customer credit for the returned material and updating the inventory record. This handling of paper and materials costs the distributor from $40 to $60 for each line item returned.

Further research has disclosed that it also costs the customer from $40 to $60 (these numbers represent the costs to large and medium-sized distributors and customers and are rounded to the nearest ten dollars). The net effect is that the actual loss to the distributor and to the customer is about $100. While this is a considerable loss it is even worse when you consider that if both the distributor and the customer were working on a four percent net profit before tax; combined they must sell $2,500 worth of products in order to make up the $100 loss.

This does not even take into account the fact that the customer may become dissatisfied with the distributor and take their business elsewhere. This indicates that the real cost may be, as Dr. W. Edwards Deming says, "unknown and unknowable." This is true because research bears out that every dissatisfied customer tells ten people about the experience while a satisfied customer tells only one.

This gives some indication of the importance of the picking and checking function.

The only acceptable solution to the error problem is the implementation of the quality process. This means that the distributor must stop thinking of business as usual and learn to change the process so that errors can be prevented, not corrected. It is borne out by research that 85 percent of errors are caused by the distributor's system and only 15 percent by the people. Therefore it is important that the distributor learn to work "on the system" to improve it so errors will be prevented. Electronic bar code scanning for instance is a helpful addition to the system because it removes much of the tedium experienced by checkers. Bar code scanning reduces the manual counting effort, increases the accuracy and provides the distributor significant labor savings as well as error reductions. The error reduction increases the customer satisfaction. Errors in the range of one per 1,000 lines of billing shipped are common with some as low as 2 - 3 per 10,000 lines of billing shipped.

Personnel Performance

One of the problems in the distributor's warehouse is the inefficiency inherent in labor-intensive areas such as picking, packing and shipping. This situation is compounded when virtually no performance measures are applied to warehouse operations by many distributors. Researchers are working diligently, using activity based costing studies to determine the cost factors and the most efficient and economical methods of performing these tasks. Better methods have been established, and distributors are being informed of the new methods so employee training can incorporate them into the learning process. More and more training will be necessary but reduction in order filling costs; zero defects and improved customer satisfaction will be the result.

Buy-outs

Occasionally, the merchandise which the customer ordered will not be available in inventory. When the customer's requirement is that the purchase order be filled complete, then it is necessary for the distributor to "buy out" that merchandise from a local competitor. This is not uncommon in the industry since customers need a full bill of materials in order to construct, manufacture, repair or maintain their products or equipment. When these buy-outs are completed, they must be coordinated with the material pulled from inventory to ship the order complete. Being sure that the buy-out material is shipped with the warehouse order is also part of the checking function.

Packing

After the merchandise is all assembled, it is ready for packing in cartons for shipment to another city, delivery to the local customer or transporting between company branches. Shipping labels designating the customer's correct address should be attached to each carton. This is most often done with computer labels.

After the boxes have been packed, the packers move them to the shipping department for shipment to out-of-town customers via freight lines, to the delivery department for local customers or to the "will-call" counter for the convenience of customers who will pick up the merchandise themselves.

This completes the sequence from purchasing to shipping. The sale has now, however, only partially been made. From an earlier discussion, it was indicated that the money must be collected from the customer and deposited in the bank before the cycle is completed. Therefore, the next discussion topics are credit, collections and cash flow.

Four

Economic Advantage, Value Added By Wholesale Distributors

Value added, or economic advantage as it is sometimes called, states the value of the functions and services performed by wholesale distributors. This is a pertinent topic for discussion because those who are not familiar with the value that distributors add often make the mistake of thinking of the distributor as a more expensive method of taking goods to market. They may also have the mistaken idea that the wholesale distributor is a "middle-man" or simply a "warehouser."

In truth, in most cases the wholesale distributor is the most economical method of marketing products to a wide range of industrial consumers. This is borne out by the rapidly increasing number of manufacturers who each year are switching from selling direct to users to selling through wholesale distributors. They do not switch to keep pace with the trend. They market through distributors because it is a better and more economical method of marketing. It also better serves customer needs. In fact, any method of distribution must be measured against the needs of consumers who want the proper product to perform a specific task available in the right quality, the right quantity, at the right time and at the optimum cost.

A discussion of the value added by wholesale distributors in serving their customers' needs follows.

Buying

First, wholesale distributors must anticipate the needs of their customers weeks, if not months, in advance in order to buy and have in inventory what the customer needs and will buy. The evaluation of the needs of customers is compiled through the history of customer buying patterns, market research on new and existing products and other marketing functions. Further consideration must be given to the seasonal variation of products such as electric fans for summer or electric heaters for winter. Ideally, if the distributor has anticipated correctly, a sufficient number of fans has been purchased to satisfy every customer demand but no fan will remain in inventory when the first heater arrives in early fall. This satisfies the needs of all customers with a minimum of inventory.

In essence, the wholesale distributor must be familiar with customer problems such as new industries entering the market, maintenance projects to be undertaken, new products being manufactured, new scientific developments and customer's needs to upgrade plants with the latest technical equipment. The distributor's salesperson, to be successful, must be a "specialist" in the customer's business.

Another buying function the distributor performs is the collection of goods from various suppliers in order to become a single source for all of these goods. This service keeps the customer from having to contact as many as 100 different manufacturers in order to put together the materials required to complete a major manufacturing project or to support an industrial, maintenance, repair, or renovation job. The ability to acquire all their goods at one location greatly simplifies the buying requirements for customers and adds value to the product by having the right product available in the right quality and quantity at the right time and at the optimum cost.

In addition, because the wholesale distributor buys larger quantities from each supplier than could most customers buying direct, many will receive a lower cost of goods through a quantity purchase "discount" which lowers the cost of goods. In addition, the distributor may receive freight allowances and cash discounts which when coupled with the quantity purchased may offset a large proportion of the gross margin of the distributor. (Gross margin is the difference between what the distributor pays for a product and what he gets for it). Freight allowance means that the manufacturer will pay the cost of shipping the product to the distributor when orders are of a specified tonnage or dollar value. Cash discounts are offered as reductions in the cost of goods as an incentive for the distributor to pay for the merchandise in a shorter than average period of time, say ten days instead of 32. This amount may be deducted from the cost of the goods and is usually one or two percent of the purchase price.

After the distributor has negotiated for the best purchase price available for the volume purchased, and carefully calculated the minimum order to get the freight paid, the order will be placed. The wholesaler purchases in full cases but sells to customers in broken lots (less than box or carton quantities) which helps the customer acquire the exact number of products needed to do the operation without purchasing a full carton or case.

The efforts of wholesale distributors to buy at the lowest cost means that their customers may also reap the benefits of the distributor's expertise and buying power. However, buying is only the first link in the value added chain. In order for the product to be of value to consumers it must be available to customers at the proper time and place.

Selling

While the distributor's buying power is primarily of benefit to the customer, its selling power is of primary benefit to its manufacturer/suppliers. The distributor which is providing the optimum service to manufacturers helps them plan their distribution strategy by providing feedback on the amount of the supplier's product which can be sold in each territory in a given time frame. Manufacturers can better plan their production schedules, sales forecasts, and market potential when consulting with wholesale distributors concerning sales forecasting.

In addition the distributor adds value by providing for both suppliers and customers a well-trained, competent sales force through which customers and potential customers are contacted frequently and with regularity. Just as the consumer would have great difficulty in buying direct from 100 or more suppliers, so would the suppliers have great difficulty calling on several thousand potential customers in a hundred major market areas. The wholesale distributor has the greatest impact for suppliers with those products that have the widest use and the most scattered market, especially with products bought frequently and in small quantities. A good example is consumable supplies which are literally used up in the manufacturing process and might include chemicals, cutting tools and abrasive, wear parts, fasteners and laminates, to mention only a few.

Even so, in a market of moderate to high technical products like those sold through wholesale distributors, probably the greatest value added for the customer's benefit is through the knowledge and expertise of highly trained salespeople who can recommend specific products which will help solve customer's problems. Buyers usually have knowledge of the problem they have, but may not have in-depth expertise to know what particular product will perform for them at the highest level of efficiency yet with the greatest return on their investment.

A buyer may understand that a certain operation can be better accomplished with a fluid power control but may not understand the advantages of investing in programmable controllers to execute the operation. At this point the salesperson helps the customer make intelligent decisions and buy the right product for that job, and, therefore, adds significant value to the product for the customer. Likewise, a good salesperson can lead a customer to change from incandescent lighting to a more efficient high pressure lighting product by showing how short a time it will take to pay for the new fixtures and their installation by savings in the amount of electricity used.

Product Availability

The production and consumption of industrial products are seldom if ever coordinated perfectly. Therefore, some storage of products is necessary until they are needed. Most wholesale distributors have warehouse facilities in close proximity to their customers so that the time lapse between demand and delivery is cut to a minimum. If distributors did not have the warehouse facilities and the required inventory, this burden would be shifted to the consumers who would have to protect themselves by having the product available in their own warehouses. When distributors perform their functions properly and consistently, customers learn to rely on their distributors to keep items in inventory for them, thus significantly cutting their costs of carrying inventory. (Annual inventory carrying costs are about 30 percent of the cost of the inventory, i.e., it costs $30,000 to store, insure, and secure $100,000 worth of inventory for one year.)

Training

The wholesale distributor's sales team (inside and outside salespeople) gets product training from the manufacturer's field sales force and from factory schools. This sales force, including the manufacturer's representatives and agents, train customers in the use of specific products, making the customer a more knowledgeable consumer. They train customers in how to use products most advantageously, how to reduce costs associated with product acquisition or possession, how to maintain products, and how to save energy with new sophisticated products.

Even so, an equally important training need arises when distributors implement the quality or continuous improvement process. Since process improvement is continuous, forever and ever, training of all the distributor's personnel must occur. Research shows that training in the range of two hours per week per person is appropriate. It is usual for the distributor who is in the quality process to have training costs of three to seven percent of operating expense.

Transportation

Transportation of a product from where it was made to where it will be used is essential to the value and thus the product's usefulness. The distributor serves two value added functions in transportation of products from manufacturer to end customer.

First, the distributor will arrange the shipping (transportation) of the product between cities. A product may be made in Los Angeles, but sold by an independent wholesale distributor in Boston. The distributor will buy in larger lots than the average consumer. The quantity purchased will generally allow him to earn a freight allowance from the manufacturer sufficient to offset the cost of transportation of the goods between cities. In any event the distributor adds value by being responsible for and arranging shipments between cities.

Secondly, the full service distributor will provide or arrange for local delivery service to the customer on both a regular scheduled delivery (every day, twice, or three times a week) as well as filling emergency delivery requests. The intracity delivery adds value to products by making materials available at the time and place of usage.

Financing

As goods are moved through the distribution channel someone must provide for the financing of these goods. Wholesale distributors are a great asset to both their manufacturer partners as well as their customers by providing financing for both.

First, the distributor is usually extended cash discounts which when taken, lower the cost of the goods to the distributor. For example, a manufacturer will offer a two percent cash discount if the distributor will pay the invoice by the 10th of the following month. By taking the cash discount and paying the bill as required, the manufacturer's cash flow is improved (it gets its money sooner). It can then reinvest in raw materials, machinery, and labor to produce more products.

Secondly, the distributor enhances the financing required by customers through extension of credit to all those who meet the distributor's credit policy requirements. Imagine the problems that would be presented to customers if they had to pay cash for every purchase, either on delivery (COD) or by going to each individual distributor and paying for merchandise before it was received. The cost of operation would be high and the efficiency severely limited. However, the distributor adds value to products by financing them, investing money in inventory before the merchandise is sold and in accounts receivable after they are sold, until the customer pays for the merchandise. This service makes products readily available to customers and improves their efficiency. This credit service adds value to products.

Some distributors get cash discounts and then offer cash discounts to their customers, even though it is usually not a good business practice to do so. (The basic rule for distributors is to take all profitable cash discounts, never give them.) Some customers offered a cash discount take them, others do not. In these cases, the financing of receivables may be of even greater value to customers who cannot or choose not to pay their bills within the discount period. When a customer does not pay for materials received for 45 to 60 days (instead of the usual 30 days) it may be because this is the only interest-free debt obtainable. In many cases it is the only financing some weaker companies can get. Therefore, most distributors are now charging their late paying customers one and one-half percent per month late charge for payments received after 30 days from the billing date.

Another economic advantage to customers is that each customer may establish credit with only a few distributors rather than many manufacturers. The distributor adds value by simplifying the credit and accounting records of both suppliers and customers.

Risk Bearing

As previously discussed, distributors finance both inventories and receivables and assume the risks associated with owning these assets. These risks would include, but not be limited to, obsolescence, deterioration, and loss through employee theft or bad debt loss. The distributor also absorbs the cost of insurance, taxes, warehousing, and handling of the inventory. These services, when utilized by customers who depend upon distributors to have inventory readily available to them, reduces the customer's cost of operation because the distributor spreads the cost of operation over all the customers served. For example, if the inventory carrying cost is 30 percent and a distributor has 100 customers all of equal size, the cost would be passed on to each one in equal shares of one percent of the total cost per customer. When you compare this to the 30 percent it would cost the customer to carry this inventory and absorb the entire cost, the saving is substantial. This adds value to the product for customers as well as suppliers who also depend upon the distributor to carry local inventory.

Market Feedback

The wholesale distributor adds further value to products sold by providing valuable information about products and their uses, market conditions, pricing information, and other factors to both suppliers and customers. This is usually not a formal research program, but is a by-product of good sales and management techniques within the distributorship by personnel who know the buying and selling functions in their market place.

In addition, salespeople can feed back to the factory information they receive from customers about the good and bad points of a product. This knowledge helps manufacturers improve products and helps customers choose the right product for specific applications.

Another service distributors provide suppliers is an estimation of sales potential for a specific product in their marketing area which adds value to the product for suppliers.

Support Staffing

Wholesale distributors maintain a staff of buyers, inventory managers, clerical assistants, technical specialists, expediters, and inside and outside sales personnel to answer product questions, provide reference materials and answer customer questions on application and availability. If this staff were employed by the manufacturer for the market place and duplicated by their customers, the cost could be excessive. The well-managed distributorship will by efficient operating procedures be able to lower their cost while keeping the customer's costs low by "spreading" the total cost over many product lines. The staffing services are provided for many manufacturers and customers; the cost of operation is lowered and shared by the spreading effect. The cost of support staff provided by distributors when properly utilized by customers is shared rather than being a duplication of cost.

Product Service

Many industrial products are prone to be complex in nature. Therefore, it is essential that adequate service be provided by the distributor for customer satisfaction. Distributor salespeople along with their manufacturer representatives and agents fulfill these needs when the customer is selecting a product. This requires that the sales team be well trained and qualified to assist customers. These sales-people in many cases are Industrial Distribution graduates, engineering graduates or seasoned field personnel.

These salespeople can also provide additional help beyond product selection by counseling customers concerning installation and even maintenance after the sale. Some distributors also provide repair and testing services as well as having spare parts available. This is a service that must be provided for customer satisfaction. If it were not provided by the distributor, it would surely be the responsibility of the manufacturers. This local service adds value to products for both suppliers and customers.

Distributor field personnel add further value to products by the knowledge they attain and have available for customers through attending various manufacturer schools and short courses, reading product literature, learning from self study materials, and from their other customers. This, coupled with years of field experience, prepares them for advising customers on improved methods of installation and application of specialty, high tech products.

Many wholesale distributors even provide engineering and pre-assembly services for design and assembly of pneumatic, hydraulic or electrical controls to fill the customer's needs for product modification before those products are shipped. All of these functions add value to the product.

Cost Savings

From the material presented concerning value added by the wholesale distributor, it should be obvious that the wide variety of functions performed by distributors assists both suppliers and customers and because the distributor works at a very low margin of profit, these services are provided very economically. In order to work within this small margin of net profit, the distributor's personnel must be excellent business people and run a very efficient operation.

The distributor's efficiency, when coupled with the ability to spread the cost of operation over many customers, makes purchasing products through wholesale distributors most advantageous for consumers of electronic components and industrial products.

Five

Choosing The Marketing Channel

There are four commonly accepted channels of distribution which a manufacturer can use to represent (sell) a product in the industrial marketplace. Each will be discussed here.

Factory Direct (Selling Direct)

From the beginning of time people have made products and sold or traded them directly to end users. This method is still used today and is practiced when a product must be specifically designed or engineered to fulfill the needs of a particular customer, e.g., large industrial machinery, machine tools for manufacturing automobiles and auto parts, certain electrical power equipment, specialty controls for chemical plants or refineries, or products for the manufacturer of heavy equipment. Selling to end users is also prevalent when large quantities of the same product are used repetitively in a limited number of locations. This happens both in original equipment manufacturer where parts are being installed in a manufactured product, as well as in some manufacturing processes where large amounts of tools or materials are being consumed in the process.

This method is referred to as "factory direct" or "selling direct" to the user and is advantageous when rigid specifications for unique equipment demand a great deal of interplay between the user and the manufacturer responsible for engineering, design, assembly, and installation. In these cases, the product is seldom made and held in inventory but is manufactured as a specialty item. Selling direct is probably the best method in this case. However, some manufacturers of motor controls, wiring devices, wire, original equipment items, and many other commodity lines also choose the factory-direct method on occasion.

However, in the past two decades the expense of selling direct in numerous geographic locations has encouraged many manufacturers to abandon this marketing method and seek more efficient ways of selling industrial products, primarily through local, independent wholesale distributors. The exceptions are those companies which do large volumes of business with only a few customers. This allows them to perform the functions described earlier and still maintain a respectable service level at a reasonable cost.

In marketing factory-direct, the manufacturer employs several people referred to as "manufacturer's representatives" or "agents," to call on customers in each marketing area and request orders for merchandise. The order, when received, is relayed to the factory (home office) for processing. The material or equipment would then be "drop shipped" (delivered from the factory, direct to the user's location). Since the representative sees the customer on only a limited basis, the service level is marginal, communication with the factory often difficult, and working out delivery schedules to fill immediate needs is difficult at best. In order to overcome these obstacles, some large and well-financed manufacturers have chosen to establish factory-owned, full service distributorships in their major market areas.

The Factory-Owned Distributorship

Some manufacturers, such as General Electric, not only manufacture electrical products, but also distribute a portion of these products to electrical users through factory-owned, full service distributorships. (The full service distributor is one who has a technically qualified sales force, keeps a large inventory, provides transportation of the materials to the user's location, extends credit and offers local service after the sale and other value added functions.)

The factory-owned wholesale distributorship establishes a wholesale outlet (warehouse, sales force, etc.) in major industrial regions where customers are to be served. Establishing distributorships in every major market area may be prohibited by cost except in a few isolated cases. Most factory-owned distributorships were established before sophisticated, full service oriented, independently owned wholesale distributors were prominent in the industrial market.

Most factory-owned wholesale distributorships will also sell complementary and noncompetitive lines of products which are supportive in nature to the products they manufacture. For example, General Electric Company manufactures and sells motor starters and controllers through their factory-owned distributor, General Electric Supply Company (GESCO). However, the electrical contractor will also need such complementary items as conduit, wire, terminals, fittings, and a host of other associated items which may not be manufactured by General Electric. Therefore, in order to be of maximum service to customers, GESCO will purchase, inventory, sell, and service these associated electrical materials along with the items manufactured by the mother company.

The Independently-Owned Wholesale Distributorship

The independent wholesale distributor is an entrepreneur (a person who organizes, operates, and accepts the risk for a business venture). When a new wholesale distributorship is to be started, one or more people join together, select from several product lines available to them, purchase an inventory with savings they have accumulated, and take the risk of selling (or not selling) the merchandise at a profit or a loss. The independent wholesale distributor, as an entrepreneur, performs all five of the standard functions: provides technical product information, maintains a local inventory, provides transportation of the product from the point of manufacture to the point of use, extends credit to the customer, services the products sold, and offers other value added services.

Unlike the factory-owned distributorship, which owes its first allegiance to the product lines manufactured by the mother company, the independent wholesale distributor is free to acquire any or all of the industrial product lines available to the company. Generally, the most highly respected distributors in a geographic territory also attract the most widely accepted product lines. Occasionally, a superior distributor will take on (agree to inventory and sell) a line which has not been strong in other areas but because of the strength of the sales team and management efforts will make that product a leader in sales in that specific region.

This freedom to seek a variety of complementary product lines (those which a customer would use together, e.g., wire and conduit, bearings and seals, cutting tools and cutting fluids) as they are available, is a part of the strength of the independent wholesale distributor. This allows the tailoring of a product mix (wide range of products) which specifically fulfills the needs of the customers these distributors serve.

Many manufacturers, however, have product lines which are not available to new distributors or those seeking to change lines or add to their product mix. For example, Allen-Bradley, a manufacturer of electrical and electronic controls has, with few exceptions, chosen to market their products in the United States through only one wholesale distributor in a given market area, which may include an entire city or metropolitan area. Once these distributorships have been chosen, it becomes extremely difficult for a competing distributor to convince Allen-Bradley to allow them to take on (have permission to inventory and sell) that product line.

On the other hand, other reputable manufacturers who sell through wholesale distributors will contract to sell through from four to seven different competing wholesale distributors in order to sell their products to all segments of a large market area. One distributor will service primarily heavy industrial accounts, another might sell to general contractors or home builders, another might sell mostly to chemical plants and refineries while yet another distributor might sell only to original equipment manufacturers. Going to market through several different types of distributors encourages sales to more market segments. The two marketing schemes are quite different, but both can be effective. These actions create a competitive spirit among the independent wholesale distributors to attract the product lines which are most often specified and requested by their customers.

Using multiple distribution in a single market can have a very detrimental effect, however, if too many distributors are appointed in a geographic region. This causes price wars which lowers profits until none of them may be interested in selling the product any more. The correct number of distributors in a market area is a very delicate balance indeed.

The Manufacturer's Representative

The manufacturer's representative (rep or factory rep) mentioned earlier also plays an important role in the marketing of industrial products through distributors.

When a manufacturer decides to market a product through a wholesale distributorship and utilize the factory staff to assist the distributor, an employee of the firm is needed to represent the company to both the distributors and the end users. This person is the factory rep and is directly responsible to the manufacturer for the sale of their products in a given geographic territory. Therefore, the rep calls on both distributors and users. Since the responsibility of the rep is to assist the local distributor, it is vital that the rep fully understand the purpose and function of the wholesale distributor, as outlined earlier in this chapter.

A rep should never consider the distributor to be the customer. The end user is the customer; the distributor is a partner. Since the two work as partners, the mutual respect of one for the other is essential. This respect or "credibility" is enhanced when the rep is technically competent, knowledgeable of the products and their applications, successful as a sales motivator, a good teacher of product knowledge to the distributor's sales team, understanding and helpful to distributors with business problems, and is a "team person."

Successful sales depend upon the teamwork which should be established between the rep and the distributor's sales team and administrative personnel. The rep should provide information for the distributor concerning potential markets and market share of the product along with the inventory it is anticipated will be required to meet the needs of potential customers.

Once the inventory is ready for sale to end users, the rep, with extensive product knowledge, should assist in the technical training of the distributor's salespeople who will also be calling on end users. In conjunction with these activities, the rep will be making individual sales calls to potential customers, purchasing managers, contractors, architects and engineers in order to get specifications of the company's products accepted by the customer.

The efforts of the manufacturer's representative are often explained as the "push-pull" system. The purpose of the rep is to "push" the distributors to put the merchandise in inventory for resale to end users. The rep and the distributor salesperson then make sales calls to industrial users, explain the value and use of the products and refer the potential customer to the distributor as the source of products. The associated sale will "pull" the merchandise from inventory. This team effort is necessary for the continuous flow of products through the distributorship.

The Manufacturer's Agent

The factory representative also has a counterpart called an "agent." Manufacturer's agents perform the same functions as do factory reps except they usually represent companies whose sales volume could not support the full salary of a representative in that market area. Therefore, agents are usually self-employed and paid on a percentage of the sales of the products they represent. The agent will usually represent eight to ten manufacturers of complementary, non-competitive products which could be sold in similar markets.

One example of a company which might choose to be represented by agents is Young Brothers Stamp Company, a manufacturer of steel stamps for stamping identifying marks on steel, aluminum or other materials. Being a small manufacturer, they cannot sustain their own factory sales forces based on the expense and their small volume of sales. Therefore, they choose to rely on the independent agent in most of their market areas. Although this company sells only through distributors, they have agents calling on both distributors and customers. These agents also represent complementary products which the Young

Brothers distributors would be likely to stock and that their customers would be likely to purchase and use.

Another example of a company which might choose to be represented by an agent would be a small electrical manufacturer who had developed and was making a wiring device for floor receptacles to meet or exceed the fire-stop capabilities for hospitals as required by the National Electrical Code. The agent has one or more local distributors which have the new receptacles in inventory. The agent not only informs the distributor salespeople concerning the technical information about the new product and makes joint sales calls with the distributor salespeople, but also calls on architects, contractors, and specifying electrical engineers in order to get the product specified in the request for bids for the new building. During the sales call the agent would also represent to the specifying engineer other product lines represented, such as energy-saving devices, specialty controls, or other lines. The agent spreads the cost of operation over all of the lines being represented. This is an important job and one which demands the ability to generate team effort toward serving customers better.

Even so, the most widely accepted role of the manufacturer's agent is that of gathering market information, providing technical product knowledge to distributors and users about where, when, why and how to best utilize the product, and supporting the sale from the distributor.

Although there is an ever-increasing number of exceptions, the agent was intended to be a non-stocking representative (keeping no inventory of products) because this is considered by many to be an infringement on, and an expensive duplication of, the services provided by the wholesale distributors. Today, more and more reps/agents are carrying a wide variety of inventory items. This duplication of warehouse space, inventory and inventory carrying costs drive up the expense unnecessarily in this channel of distribution.

Marketing Channels for Industrial Products

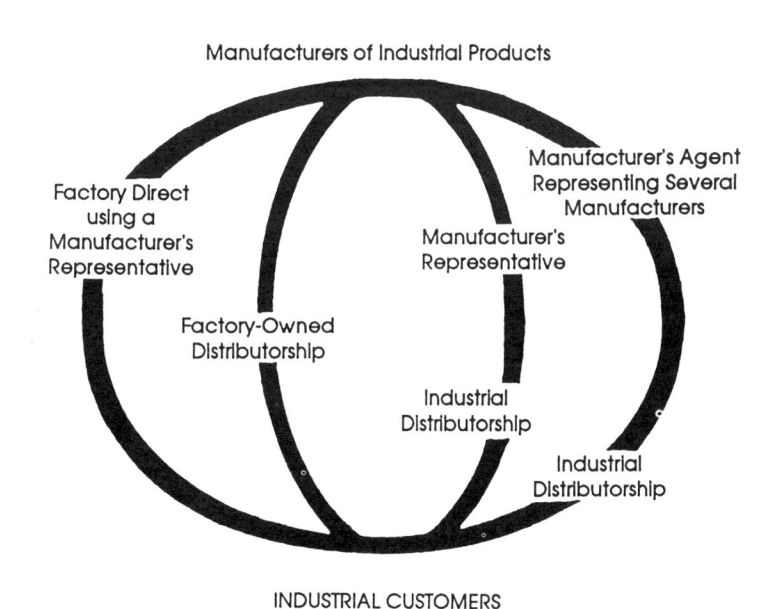

Manufacturers of Industrial Products

Factory Direct using a Manufacturer's Representative

Manufacturer's Agent Representing Several Manufacturers

Manufacturer's Representative

Factory-Owned Distributorship

Industrial Distributorship

Industrial Distributorship

INDUSTRIAL CUSTOMERS

Six

The Role Of The Manufacturer

As more and more manufacturers choose to go to market through wholesale distributors, a general definition of the responsibilities of both parties should be discussed. If the distributor and manufacturer are to operate as a team, each should know what to expect from the other. A general overview of these expectations will be presented. The legal and technical details of the working relationship will be left for another discussion. The functions the distributor performs have been examined. The functions of the manufacturer will be discussed here.

The first responsibility of the manufacturer is to make a quality product which fulfills the requirements of the application. The demands for quality vary accordingly. A pneumatic impact wrench used occasionally in a tire repair or mechanics shop will not need to be of the same quality and durability as one which is used continuously during an assembly line operation, as in the manufacture of automobiles. Some manufacturers make tools of different quality (and price) in order to cover both markets. Others will choose to be active in only one market. It is important that the manufacturer know the market for which the product is being produced, make products which meet the requirements of that market, and offer them for sale through distributors at a competitive price.

An example of this wide variation would be the manufacturer of welding equipment and associated supplies for limited service use, e.g., for farmers and light industrials as compared to pipeline or heavy industrial equipment. Another example would be compressed air equipment which has a wide variety of uses from the farm shop to the large industrialist. The compressor for the industrial application would need to be much more durable than would one for farm utilization. Each manufacturer must make and sell equipment within the market for which it is intended.

Although the primary responsibility of the wholesale distributor is to provide a local inventory of products, the manufacturer also should make every effort to keep sufficient inventory to fill distributor's orders, if not quickly, at least consistently. The ability of the distributor to count on consistent lead times from manufacturers is necessary for good customer service. (Lead time is the time required to place an order, wait for delivery, and place the item in inventory ready for shipment to consumers.) If lead times are consistent, whether they be long or short, the distributor can plan accordingly and have inventory on the shelf when the customer needs it. However, fluctuating lead times are detrimental to providing satisfactory customer service.

Another responsibility of the manufacturer is to create a market for their products through advertising. Advertisements in new product magazines and trade journals read by potential customers provide the consumer with knowledge of the product, its advantages and what it can be expected to accomplish. This product identity makes sales calls by the distributor salespeople more productive, because purchasing people are more apt to be familiar with the name and quality if they have seen the new product and its applications advertised.

Advertisements in trade journals and new product magazines will bring product inquiries to the manufacturer's address. These should be forwarded to the distributor so that follow-up calls can be made quickly.

Many times manufacturers send sales leads from advertisements to both the distributors and to the manufacturer's rep working that territory. If the request is for information about a new product, the rep can make a joint call with the distributor salesperson to insure that proper technical back-up is provided. The factory rep is also made available by the manufacturer to the distributors, and many times even to contractors and users, to provide training seminars on proper design, utilization, installation, and maintenance of technical products. The rep should provide these as a regular service, but should also be available to the distributor on a "call" basis, to help with immediate technical problems. In the event that the rep cannot solve customer problems in the field, factory engineers should be made available for assistance.

Another responsibility of the manufacturer is to print catalogs which clearly describe their products, including material, dimension, utilization, etc., for both customers and their wholesale distributors. This allows purchasing managers, buyers, engineers, and maintenance people to look up and compare one product with another and make intelligent decisions with a minimum of effort.

The manufacturer should also participate in trade shows and expositions where products are open to inspection by potential customers. Most trade associations have these on a regular basis. Some examples are the Offshore Technology Conference, The Machine Tool Builders Exposition and the National Home Builders Conference. The people participating in the manufacturer's booths at these shows should be steeped in both technical knowledge and product applications. Sales leads gathered during the show should be forwarded to the distributors covering that geographic territory for follow-up. Any orders received by the factory as a result of the show, or other advertisement, should also be sent to the local distributor.

It is important to the distributor that the manufacturer provide every legal means within state and federal laws to provide the distributor with a guarded territory. A guarded territory protects a local distributor from investing time, talent, and financial resources in helping a customer solve a problem by the proper application of a product yet have another distributor for the same manufacturer but from another geographic area make the lowest bid and receive the order when no service was provided. This is not that uncommon. A customer may call a local wholesale distributor for assistance with the control of a manufacturing process. The distributor salesperson may recommend, after a great deal of time and research, that one particular product will best solve the problem. Occasionally the buyer will then send out a call for bids specifying that product. The order may then be awarded to the lowest bidder, usually someone other than the one who assisted in the recommendation, because that bidder has no funds invested in consultation. This is unfair to the original distributor who furnished the design work.

The manufacturers who realize the value added by their distributors should be open to suggestions for improvement in their relationship and operating policies and procedures. As this marketing partnership is strengthened, more manufacturers are establishing "Distributor Advisory Committees" made up of leading distributor executives who have been instrumental in promoting their products in the marketplace. As they share ideas they learn more about each other's operations and how they can help one another grow and become more prosperous without adding to the financial burdens of the other--a true partnership.

One of the priorities of the manufacturer should be to establish and publish distributor-oriented policies which commit the manufacturer to long term relationships with their wholesale distributors.

Thomas & Betts, a manufacturer of wire terminals and associated electrical products, has such a policy which is printed in this chapter. (Reprinted by Permission of Thomas & Betts, Memphis, TN). This comprehensive distributor policy was strengthened by a challenge issued to T&B by the armed forces during World War II, to demonstrate that selling products through distributors, rather than selling "direct," actually saved the U.S. Government money. The excerpts presented here are taken from the letter of reply from T&B to the armed forces which was reprinted in the October 1951 issue of <u>Electrical Wholesaling</u>. The message they sent to the armed forces in 1945 is still true today. This letter is worth reading carefully.

THE T&B PLAN
OF
WHOLESALE DISTRIBUTION

More than 65 years experience has convinced us that Wholesale Distribution reduces the Manufacturer's selling cost and thereby reduces the selling price of their products to the user. Therefore, our policy has been to market our products exclusively through the Wholesale Distributor.

In 1937, we evolved The Plan, the objective of which is to strengthen our Distributor's position with the users of electrical and electronic products, because anything we can do to help him, helps us. To accomplish the objectives of The Plan, we will continue to advertise to the user the value of the many services performed by the Distributor. Through all means at our command, we will communicate our policies and demonstrate the underlying economic reasons for those policies.

T. Kevin Dunnigan
T. Kevin Dunnigan
PRESIDENT

The following points implement The Plan in action:

1 We will constantly demonstrate the economies of the Wholesale Distributor's services to his customers through national advertising integrated with general promotion.

2 We will — without exception — bill T&B/Thomas & Betts material only to our authorized Distributors.

3 We maintain a One Price Policy — without discrimination in any form.

4 We maintain a liberal Return Goods Policy. Under the conditions outlined in published terms, we will grant permission for the return of any T&B/Thomas & Betts standard catalog items, which have been shipped to Distributors' stocks, for full merchandise credit or exchange, without service or freight charges.

5 We offer a liberal Price Protection Policy. Any price reductions published by T&B/Thomas & Betts will be retroactive to include shipments made to Distributors' stocks since and including the first day of the preceding calendar month.

6 We will make available to our Distributor materials to promote his products and re-emphasize the Distributor's essential services. T&B/Thomas & Betts will also build demand for its products through national advertising.

7 We will help you compete with direct-selling manufacturers by making the services of the T&B Engineering Department a part of your organization on "special" as well as standard customer requirements.

8 Our salesmen are directed to help our Distributor's personnel with product sales meetings, inventory control, technical advice, missionary sales calls, and other marketing functions.

9 We will constantly maintain the highest quality products through recognized statistical quality control methods to meet Codes and recognized standards.

10 We will continue to pioneer in developing new products for new uses. We will also continue to redesign products and improve manufacturing methods for maximum product improvement.

11 We will keep price information, catalogs, packaging and labels up-to-date at all times.

12 We recognize the need for close management communication between the Distributor and the Manufacturer and will encourage and provide the opportunity for Management-to-Management meetings.

March 6, 1945

Gentlemen:

You have requested that we give you, in writing, the basic economic principles underlying our principle of doing all of our business through our electrical distributors. We greatly appreciate the opportunity to present our reasoning to you, and we are submitting this with the understanding that it will be used as a basis for discussion only; and that no unfavorable decision will be reached without giving us an opportunity to appear personally.

***

In considering whether or not the services of a distributor shall be recognized, it should first be determined and recognized that there are certain "distribution costs" over and above the labor, material and overhead costs of production. The only sound claim to recognition is that the distributor can, and does, <u>perform the distribution functions</u> (described below), <u>less expensively</u> than anyone else can, and this is the only reason for his survival in the competitive business world.

We have frequently heard the expression that "paying the distributor a profit is paying a double profit." We are completely convinced, and we intend to demonstrate, that this contention is a fallacy. The distribution functions (which we detail later) must be performed by someone, and paid for. If we, as manufacturers, perform them, we are entitled to their cost, plus our profit. If the distributor, especially organized to perform them, does so less expensively than we could, then the cost plus profit is less than our cost plus our profit, and the purchaser benefits by this saving.

***

Almost 50 years of experience in our business has convinced us that wholesaler distribution, to which we have adhered <u>consistently for 25 years, without any exception</u> - that is, turning over the distribution functions of our business to electrical wholesalers, reduces the selling price of our goods to the user, Government or private. Our experience with war production and our cost studies for renegotiation purposes simply strengthen this conviction.

We are organized to do business with customers who perform for us, cheaper than we could ourselves, the essential distributor functions of our business. The distribution functions include:

1. Warehousing at point of requirement.

2. Selling—and providing technical information.

It is not necessary to "sell" the Government, but essential dissemination of technical and catalog information by our local distributors reduces our cost for this item, and eliminates annoying and costly delays to the Government.

3.   Financing and extending credit.

This company has <u>no Government money or loans</u>. It operates entirely on its own capital and credit and is <u>not seeking to establish a business at the Government's expense</u>.

We are able to operate a comparatively large business on comparatively small capital, because our distributors act as bankers, utilizing their own capital to extend Government credit, while paying us every 15 days, thus enabling us to meet increased payroll and inventory obligations. Through unavoidable complications and technicalities, the Government can, and does frequently, hold up payments. Our distributors carry these accounts for us. We know of many cases where we have received our money promptly from the distributor, whereas the distributor wasn't paid for up to nine months.

4.   Transacting detail customer business.

    a.   Executing quotations and forms.
    b.   Posting bonds, computing freight charges, etc.
    c.   Handling claims, credits, shortages on the spot.
    d.   Billing and following shipments.
    e.   Collecting.

The Government has thousands of local supply procurement, and disbursing offices, etc., all doing business (procuring, receiving, and settling,) with contractors. The Government has found it expedient and economical to localize these functions. So must the Government contractor localize, in order to handle specifications, quotations, forms, bonds, credits, claims, collections, etc., of all the local Government offices.

There seem to be only three (3) alternatives by which the contractor can do local business.

1. By traveling representatives from his plant.
2. By establishing his own complete local offices.
3. By utilizing the existing, competent, and strategically located services of distributors.

The first method has generally been found impractical for obvious physical and expense reasons. The second, branch office method, may be justified as economical where consistent local volume is great enough to support its cost. But the third method is the only apparent economical solution for plants of medium or small volume, whose sources of business are varied and inconsistent, for the reason that the cost of these local functions remains consistent with the local volume, when the distributors established services are utilized, as required.

Further, the local distributor reduces the cost of his services to any one manufacturer by spreading his total cost over the products of all the manufacturers for whom he performs these functions.

In our own office, we handle credit and collections of our customers with half a girl's time, and our billing with a very small group. To add thousands of new and strange accounts, and to bill and follow them, would require a tremendous expansion of our office force simply to duplicate our distributors existing facilities at great added expense to us and the Government. We would have to add a claims department, now handled as routine by means of our distributor's reports. Over and above the added expense, and therefore cost to the Government, of selling direct, we believe it to be practically physically impossible to expand either our offices or office force sufficiently under present critical conditions.

***

To summarize and illustrate what we have said, if your department will go back through its experience with competitive invitations to bids issued by its procurement offices, it will find that this company, by utilizing the economical services of our distributors, has received its full share, or more, of competitive Government bidding against manufacturers who quote the Government direct. For your information, this has been equally true in private commercial bidding. For 25 years, both the Government and private users have been able to procure

Thomas & Betts material through our distributors at equal or less cost than they could consistently procure equivalent material direct from other sources. Naturally, we are completely convinced that our method of conducting our business is economically sound and right. At least, in our case, we trust you will agree.

***

Very truly yours,
THE THOMAS & BETTS COMPANY, INC.
N. J. MacDonald, V. P.

(Reprinted by Permission, Thomas & Betts, Memphis, TN)

This explanation satisfied the Government that the functions performed by the electrical distributor are both essential and economical. Each distributor should take time to teach the management staff and employees that the functions which they perform for the manufacturer are important to both suppliers and consumers and that profits made are justifiable for the services performed.

The manufacturer likewise should inform the sales and management personnel of the services the distributors are providing for the company. Due respect for the value added to the product should be recognized by both parties of the partnership.

The manufacturer should also acknowledge as well as pay for the value the distributor adds to the products by the service provided. This is enhanced when the partners can agree on the quality of the product and service required by the customer, returned goods policies, freight allowances, small or special orders, and the limits of product liability to be assumed by each. These policies should not be bent in favor of one or the other, but be mutually agreeable to both parties. Neither party should intentionally or arbitrarily conduct business in such a manner as to increase the operating costs of the other or to the end user.

The manufacturer should also allow the distributor sufficient discounts from trade price (what the item was sold to the customer for) so that the gross margin would allow the distributor to earn a reasonable profit. (The difference between what the distributor paid for an item and what was received in payment is the gross margin.) For most industrial distributors, for every $100 in sales $98 will be spent on the cost of goods sold and the cost of doing business. Two dollars or less will represent the net profit. At the same time the manufacturer should expect the distributor to be efficient in business operations and thus earn the gross margin and the profit made available.

Seven

Why Contractors And Industrial Users Buy From Wholesale Distributors

The question, "Why buy from a wholesale distributor?" often arises because buyers and purchasing managers are not fully informed about the advantages of purchasing goods from this source. Since the shortest distance between two points is a straight line, or so it seems, some suggest the most logical method of purchasing products would be directly from the manufacturer. This may be true for most of the raw materials which a company uses in making a product for sale since approximately 20 percent of the time of a purchasing manager's staff is spent buying 80 percent of the dollar volume of materials. This percentage includes the raw materials and capital equipment required to manufacture a product and is an economical buying ratio. However, the reverse ratio implies that 80 percent of the purchasing manager's time is spent buying only 20 percent of the dollar volume of goods and services needed, which is not an economical ratio.

This lopsided figure, as shown on the following page, is not cost effective. The problem is that it is generally known from week to week what raw materials and machinery will be needed to manufacture a product, but what about the maintenance, repair and operations (MRO) items needed to keep the plant operational? It is not uncommon for a large manufacturing firm to purchase as many as 20,000 different MRO items during the course of a year's operations, e.g., motors, drives, controls, electronic components, abrasives, welding metals and gasses, bearings, pumps and pump parts, industrial rubber goods, fasteners and fluid power products, to mention only a few items.

Why Buy From an Electrical Distributor?

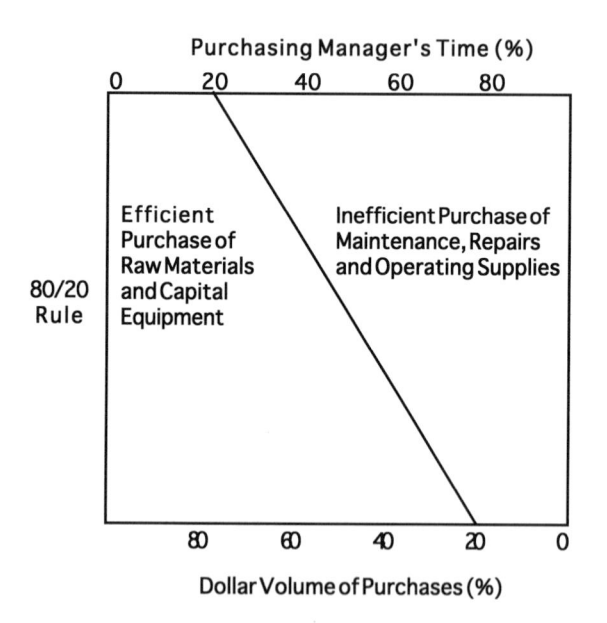

```
                Purchasing Manager's Time (%)
           0      20      40      60      80
         ┌─────────────────────────────────────┐
         │                                     │
         │   Efficient        Inefficient Purchase of │
         │   Purchase of      Maintenance, Repairs    │
         │   Raw Materials    and Operating Supplies  │
 80/20   │   and Capital                       │
 Rule    │   Equipment                         │
         │                                     │
         │                                     │
         └─────────────────────────────────────┘
             80      60      40      20      0
                Dollar Volume of Purchases (%)
```

These are low volume, low dollar items but purchasing requires a great deal of time and technical expertise in order to obtain the exact product needed for the application. These MRO items are the same items which the wholesale distributor keeps in inventory. Visualize for a moment a vast chemical complex of pipes, vessels, gauges, and instrumentation such as the ones built by DuPont, Dow, Union Carbide, Shell and Monsanto. Each of these units could quite easily consume 25,000 or more different MRO products made by 250 different manufacturers each year. Imagine the manpower and paperwork which would be required to purchase all of these items directly from the 250 different manufacturers. The chart below shows the lines of communication required for the five companies named above to purchase products from only five of the 250 manufacturers of MRO supplies.

MANUFACTURERS

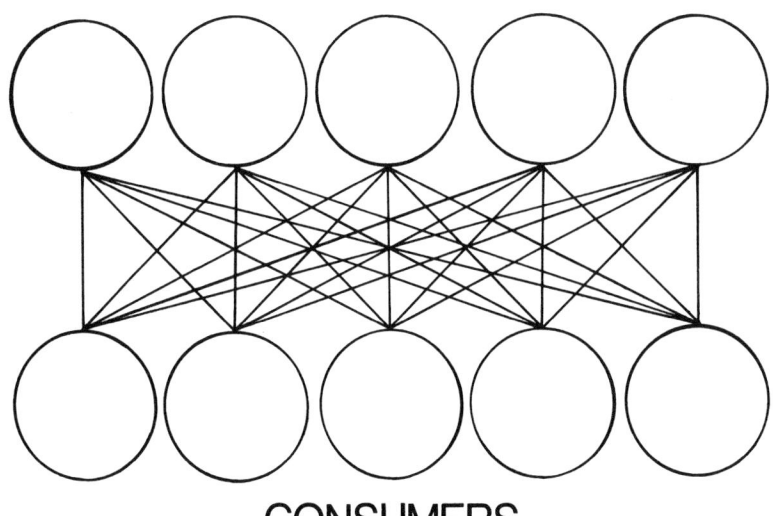

CONSUMERS

The same thing is true for residential and industrial contractors and the equipment they install in homes, commercial, and industrial plant sites. Imagine how hectic it would be if the contractors purchasing manager had to purchase all of the products and equipment needed to build an apartment complex, equip a large refinery, an electronic component manufacturing and assembly facility, or a plastics manufacturing plant, when the products were made by even 50 different manufacturers in 25 or 30 cities. This situation is even worse when you consider that only a few items may be needed to finish up the job but have to be ordered direct from the factory and it takes several weeks for the products to arrive. Delays of this type are common and the expense excessive when purchasing direct from the factory. This is another reason industrial contractors buy from local distributors.

As you can tell, buying direct from manufacturers can be a complicated and hectic arrangement. The problem is compounded when the actual number of contacts, 16 per purchase, is considered. A typical example is a company needing several safety items for use by personnel in the plant. Twenty different safety items are requested by the safety engineer. These include electronic instruments which detect the presence of combustible gasses, respirators, safety eye protection, protective clothing and protective head wear, to mention only a few items needed. The company has decided to purchase these items direct from the manufacturers.

The communication process begins when four letters are mailed to leading manufacturers along with a request for bids for the products which are needed. Hopefully, more than one manufacturer will make all of the product, although it is highly unlikely. This would eliminate the need for additional bidding or splitting the order between two or more companies. The competition should also make the price more competitive. In this example, let's assume that four requests were sent out and three bids were submitted, complete. One of the bids is accepted and an order is placed. The merchandise is received and placed in inventory in the user's warehouse. The delivery receipt is matched with the invoice to determine if the merchandise received was what was ordered. Inventory records and disbursements of the materials must be posted with the receipt. One or more notes or phone calls to expedite (speed up) the progress of the order will be needed before the entire order is received and the invoice has been cleared for payment. By purchasing directly from the manufacturer, the average company which chooses to purchase by this method will experience 16 contacts for each order processed.

This is a very expensive method of purchasing MRO supplies or construction materials. Frustration and possible productivity loss by employees who do not have the necessary supplies on hand to finish the job must also be considered. The misleading element in this process is the illusive word, "price." In this example, the price may be lower than the price quoted by a local distributor. However, when all the "cost" factors have been weighed, it is usually more cost effective to pay a slightly higher price, but lower the total cost of acquiring and owning MRO supplies.

Because of the free enterprise economy in America, a better system has been developed for purchasing contractor and MRO items. This method is to purchase supplies through the local wholesale distributor. The basic principle of purchasing through distributors is quite simple. The following graph depicts the lines of communication required when one distributor purchases inventory from five manufacturers and sells them to five consumers.

MANUFACTURERS

DISTRIBUTOR

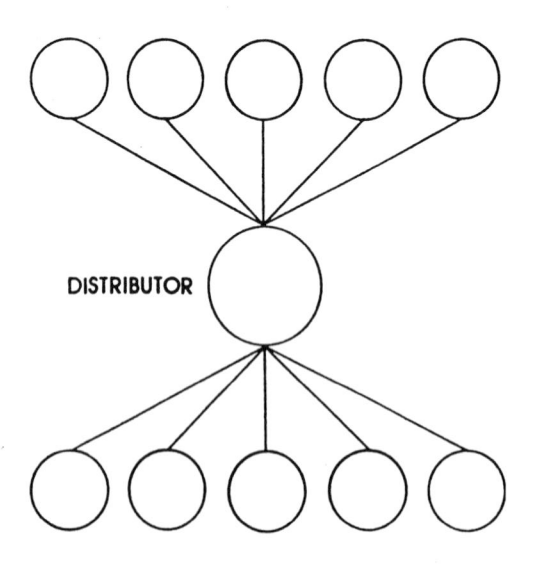

CONSUMERS

There is a significant difference between the simplicity of this graph and the complexity of the one showing five consumers buying directly from five manufacturers. The difference shown is a real difference and is a strong argument for purchasing from wholesale distributors.

There are many other advantages in buying from the wholesale distributor. One of these is the reduction of purchasing costs. It is true that the distributor also experiences purchasing costs, as does the user buying direct. However, because the distributor sells the products purchased to many users, the cost of purchasing <u>is spread</u> over all of the customers who purchase these products. This is coupled closely with the advantage the distributor has of buying more products because the purchase is made for many customers.

This allows the distributors to buy more of each item each time an order is placed. Purchasing in bulk not only reduces the cost to purchase each item, it probably entitles the distributor to a <u>quantity discount</u>. (A quantity discount is a reduction in the cost of goods and is allowed because the purchase of larger amounts on one order reduces the manufacturer's costs of handling the order.) The quantity discount lowers the cost of goods and thus helps keep the costs down for consumers. In contrast, the consumer purchasing direct pays all of the costs required to purchase and may or may not be entitled to a quantity discount.

The contractor or industrial user will still have purchasing expense, even when buying from the distributor, but because distributors keep from 200 to 50,000 items or more in inventory, the number of purchase orders can be reduced, thus lowering the user's cost of purchasing.

The advantage of working out of another company's inventory is also significant in purchasing from the wholesale distributor. Wise consumer management will reduce their own company inventories by depending upon the stock held by the local distributor. This reduces the user's warehouse expense and lowers operating costs. Consumers can reduce their inventories because reliable distributors know what their customer's use and keep that merchandise in stock in order to meet their customer's immediate needs.

This is an important concept and its application requires team effort. Consumers who are in "the quality process" share usage information with distributors and find that the distributor is better able to fulfill their material and service requirements. Unfortunately, until recent years industrial buyers were reluctant to buy from a single source or to share usage information with suppliers. However, the increased costs of doing business in a global economy has more or less forced consumers to actively seek a "partnership" arrangement with distributors as they try to lower their operating costs. This openness about quality and usage requirements will continue to enhance the distributors service to the user and will continue to bring about significant cost savings for both parties.

As the user depends more upon the inventories held by a limited number of distributors, a marked difference will be made in the users cost to own these inventories. As interest and tax rates rise, wise buyers lower the amount of inventory held in their warehouses because it costs money to own merchandise. For example, the local taxing authorities in many areas assess taxes on inventories. The more inventory owned, the more taxes paid. If money was borrowed to purchase the inventory, interest must be paid on the loan. Even if money had not been borrowed to buy the inventory, if the inventory is reduced, the money not spent on interest can be reinvested in materials, machinery or new construction projects, which could bring returns on the investment. Even if none of these were true there is still the "lost value" of the money because the user could not even earn interest in a savings account when the money was tied up in unnecessary inventory.

The next question becomes, "How much can you afford to buy?" This simple diagram explains the concept of economic order quantity, or "cost to buy" versus "cost to own." It is true that the more products that are bought on a single purchase order and shipped at one time, the lower the percent cost to purchase each item.

ECONOMIC ORDER QUANTITY

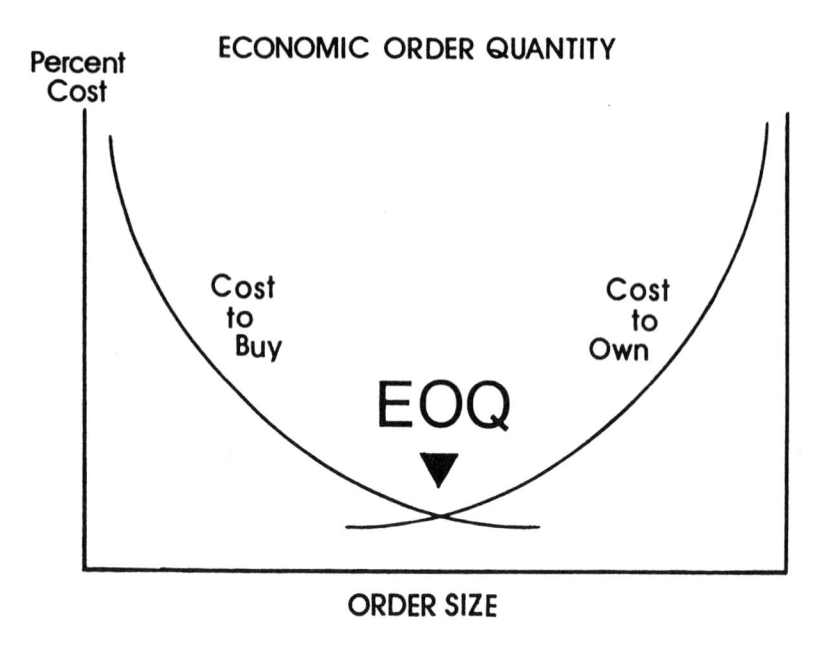

```
Percent
 Cost


          Cost                Cost
           to                  to
          Buy                 Own

                  EOQ
                   ▼

              ORDER SIZE
```

Example:

If it costs a company $100 to cut and handle a purchase order, and $100 worth of materials are purchased on that order, then the cost to buy is equal to the cost of the merchandise, and the total cost will be $200. As the dollar value of the merchandise increases with the larger order size, the cost of the purchase order remains constant, but the percentage cost to buy decreases. If $1,000 worth of materials is purchased on an order which costs $100 to process, the cost to buy decreases to only 10 percent of the total order cost.

In the EOQ example the curve on the left depicts the "cost to buy" each item. The "cost to own" curve is on the right. The more items owned, the higher the cost to own them. Some of these costs are interest, taxes, insurance, personnel and warehouse space.

It is easy to see that the consumers of industrial products who rely on distributors can lower operating costs by depending upon the distributor's inventory. The more items purchased on one purchase order, the lower the cost to buy each item. However, the more items purchased, the higher the cost to own that merchandise. Somewhere between these two extremes is an area known as the Economic Order Quantity (EOQ) which should be calculated before supplies are purchased.

Another reason users rely on wholesale distributors for inventory is that it reduces obsolescence (number of products which become obsolete because of outmoded design or uselessness). When contractors and industrial users buy direct from the manufacturer, products are more often purchased in case lots. Before the entire case is used, a new product may come on the market which renders the old product obsolete. Another reason for obsolescence is that a product design or process may be changed and no longer require a particular item. The remainder of the case must then be discarded at an economic loss. However, when the user purchases from a local distributor, merchandise may be purchased as needed, and in a quantity consistent with the number of items to be installed or consumed in the process.

Electrical relays are a good example. Relays are being replaced by solid state electronic devices, like programmable controllers or computers. This parallels closely the way vacuum tubes became obsolete with the introduction of the transistor. A company which purchased large numbers of relays and had them in stock as repair parts for replacement purposes found that they had obsolete inventory on hand when the plant engineers recommended that they be replaced by programmable controllers or computers.

Another advantage of purchasing through wholesale distributors is that the waiting time is reduced. It may take several weeks or even months to receive an order direct from the factory, but most distributors deliver to their contractor and industrial customers daily. Service minded distributors deliver to all parts of major cities each working day and some twice a day, as well as providing "hot shots" (emergency delivery service) on special request. An order placed in the morning will be delivered the next working day by most distributors.

Where purchasing personnel have entered into the quality process, have limited the number of distributors they purchase from, and have shared usage information with these distributors, it is not uncommon for 97 percent of an order to be filled from stock and shipped for delivery within 24 hours or less. This service is excellent and essential for the purchase of materials and supplies needed to keep a plant operational.

Industrial consumers may find that purchasing their MRO supplies through wholesale distributors rather than direct from manufacturers frees buyers and purchasing management to conduct studies on usage patterns and buying habits which result in even greater savings. Occasionally, the purchasing staff can be reduced. This reduction occurs because the number of qualified products and suppliers (cleared by management as a dependable, quality product or dependable supplier) can be minimized. Instead of working with 100 different manufacturers, the consumer is in contact with only six or seven local distributors. This process of "vendor reduction" is an essential part of the quality process because it limits the variability between products and suppliers.

Most large wholesale distributors offer their customers what they consider "one-stop shopping" for many industrial goods. Companies could theoretically purchase all of their supplies from a single source. Briggs-Weaver, a leading wholesale distributor chain, has a wide variety of industrial goods in their inventory. In order to see the significance of this service, imagine a homemaker trying to prepare dinner without a supermarket. This would require a trip to the dairy for milk, the butcher for meat, and the produce vendor for vegetables.

Sound ridiculous? Of course it does. So is the concept of buying industrial supplies direct from manufacturers when local distributors provide a wide range of products in stock like a supermarket. The manufacturer or contractor can usually purchase all of the products needed at one Briggs-Weaver location because they are a full service wholesale distributor.

The purchasing manager's staff, which purchases from a reduced number of local wholesale distributors, will have fewer quotations to handle, fewer invoices to write, check and confirm, and fewer orders to expedite because many different types of items can be purchased from the distributor on a single purchase order. Expediting is also easier because the number of companies and invoices have been reduced and expediters become familiar with local people who are more service oriented. This cuts through bottlenecks and red tape and gets products delivered sooner to the location where they are needed, with significantly fewer errors and at a significantly lower cost.

Savings are also realized in other areas, such as receiving and inventory management. Since supplies are being delivered from only a few local distributors, the chances for delivery errors are reduced. Local drivers learn where and when the user likes to have certain merchandise delivered, especially in large plants or construction sites.

Also, keeping records of service levels (how well the distributor is performing as measured against customer requirements) on only a few distributors should not be overlooked as a savings. It certainly is advantageous to the customer in terms of time and effort to repeatedly purchase from the distributor who delivers 100 percent of the product as specified 100 percent of the time (or close to it), and bills the materials out correctly. For this reason, savings are also realized in paying fewer accounts. It is not uncommon for a two percent error (two errors per 100 lines of billing) to cost the distributor 25 to 40 percent of the operating expense for that branch. There is a similar expense for these errors borne by the customer. That is why more users are reducing the number of vendors they purchase from and choosing only those which are in the quality process and have errors of only one in 1,000 lines of billing or less.

What does all of this mean to the construction superintendent or the plant manager? Would you believe an improvement in efficiency, fewer personnel, lower inventories, reduced waiting time and obsolescence, and lower maintenance costs? Most purchasing managers realize that a dollar saved in purchasing makes the same contribution to the company's net profit as $20 in sales at five percent net profit before taxes. This knowledge stimulates the buyer to want to purchase on "price." However, what is significantly more important is "cost." <u>Every dollar saved in overhead or other expenses of buying or owning supplies makes the same contribution to net profit as do savings in purchasing</u>.

A cost comparison analysis between buying direct from the manufacturer and buying from local wholesale distributors should prove very interesting when all of the factors of lost production and down-time from lack of an industrial item are included along with the other savings mentioned above. It is not the price but the total cost which is considered by professional industrial purchasing managers. This is why they purchase supplies from local wholesale distributors, with the greatest emphasis being on those who have embraced and been successful in implementing the quality process, because they will be the low cost, hassle-free provider of goods and services.

Eight

Why Manufacturers Market Products Through Wholesale Distributors

The moving of an industrial product down the line of distribution from the point of manufacture to the point of use requires certain functions to be performed. The question that arises is, "Who can best perform these functions?" A few manufacturers still believe that they can manufacture a product, warehouse it in a local market, provide the sales and technical expertise for local customers, extend credit, provide transportation, and service the product after the sale economically. In cases where only a few large consumers are located in a small geographic area (auto makers in Detroit), and where only a few expensive units of a specialized nature are made, this method of marketing works quite well. However, for the bulk of the industrial products which are manufactured for sale and use in building homes, commercial buildings, factories and industrial plants, the principle of the manufacturer marketing directly to end users and providing all of the necessary functions fails to accomplish the intended purpose. An examination of the marketplace and the financial restraints will explain this view.

A manufacturer makes a wide range of products for sale to several different sizes and types of contractors or industrial consumers. While there is a wide range of products within the line, the line itself may be quite narrow, as the following example concerning adhesives and adhesive-related products will show. The materials might be manufactured for use in the bonding (gluing) of a wide range of materials in the manufacturing or construction process. A good example would be the bonding together of the two halves of a hand-held calculator after the electronic components have been installed, or the lamination of a plastic material to a counter top in a store or family residence. A significant difference in the types and chemical design of adhesive materials is required to fulfill the needs of manufacturers and contractors because they use a wide variety of raw materials. These range from wood and other natural materials to space age plastics, ceramics and other man-made materials and fibers. Adhesive tape is another product which has wide utilization in industry and would be made by some adhesive manufacturers. These materials would be used for assembly, packaging, electrical insulation, construction and numerous other industrial and construction applications. The objective of adhesive manufacturers is to sell their products in this wide variety of markets.

In order to cover all major market segments by selling direct, a manufacturer must maintain a large sales force of personnel calling on several segments of the industry. This is very expensive. However, when the manufacturer chooses to go to market through wholesale distributors, the distributor's sales force is familiar with and already calling on most of those contractors and industrial customers. The sales expense is less per sale because the distributor salesperson's salary and expenses are not taken from the sale of only one product line, but are spread over the entire spectrum of goods sold. The distributor's personnel, because of their knowledge of local markets and the fact that they would be calling on more market segments, should provide the manufacturer with greater market share and penetration than could be realized through factory salespeople alone.

Another very important factor in marketing an industrial product is cash flow. Cash flow is the regular movement of cash (money) from the bank into raw materials which are then manufactured into finished products and sold, and credit extended. When the goods are paid for, almost all of the cash is reinvested into raw materials, labor costs, energy sources and physical facilities. The cash circulates (flows) around and around. Obviously, the longer it takes a product to be made and sold and the money collected, the more money the manufacturer must invest in order to finance all of the business operations. When a product does not sell quickly, or the purchaser does not pay for the materials quickly, then more cash must be borrowed or be put into the company by the stockholders or owner to provide the operating capital needed to run the business.

Another cause of cash flow problems is tight money. When interest rates rise, some customers take longer to pay their bills. When the manufacturer has difficulty collecting accounts receivable (the monies owed by distributors or customers), additional money must be acquired as shown above.

There is an alternative to this cash flow problem. When a manufacturer chooses to go to market through wholesale distributors, the distributor purchases the merchandise and pays for it in the course of normal business operations, usually 10 to 30 days. This process shortens the cash flow cycle because the last piece of merchandise does not have to be sold to the eventual consumer before the money is received. This is because the distributor will usually purchase a two months supply of the product to be sold and will pay for the items shortly after purchase, not when they are sold. This considerably enhances the cash flow situation for the manufacturer. Cash flow is so important that many manufacturers offer their distributors cash discounts (an amount which may be deducted from the bill) if the invoice is paid within a specified time, usually 10 to 30 days.

For example, a distributor purchases oil field country tubular goods from a manufacturer and is invoiced (sent a bill) for $200,000. The manufacturer, seeking to improve the cash flow, marks the invoice, under terms of the sale, "2% 10th prox, net 30th." This means that two percent of the amount of the invoice can be <u>deducted</u> if the bill is paid by the 10th of the following month. This would mean a saving to the distributor of .02 x $200,000 = $4,000. The distributor would deduct this amount and send the manufacturer a check for $196,000 by the 10th of the month following the month in which the bill was presented.

Well-managed distributorships take the cash discounts offered even when money is tight because it builds a good credit rating and working relationship with the manufacturer and is also profitable. Some distributors who take their cash discounts will save as much money as they will make in net profit on the sale of the goods.

Another advantage of selling through wholesale distributors is order size. Several manufacturers have rather large minimum order sizes, either by weight (as in steel or castings) or by dollar volume (in smaller or more expensive products). The average distributor will usually purchase sufficient inventory of that product to cover anticipated sales for 60 to 75 days, all on one order. This would allow the distributor to buy and sell the product (one inventory turn) five or six times annually. The distributors order would be considerably larger than one received from an end user buying direct, which obviously would drive up the manufacturer's cost of doing business. Larger orders reduce the overhead for the manufacturer, make the company more profitable, and allow for more competitive pricing. This method of marketing allows manufacturers to do what they do best -- "design and manufacture quality products." The sale and distribution of the products is then left to the professionals, the local wholesale distributor.

Another problem faced by manufacturers who sell direct is inventory control: making and having in the warehouse what the customer needs at the time it is needed, which is known as "just-in-time inventory control." If sufficient inventory is available at the factory to fulfill all of the customer's needs at the time the order is placed, extremely high inventory costs will be incurred. The alternative is to set up and manufacture what the customer needs if it is not in stock. The problem here is machinery set-up time. This is the time it takes to change machinery from making one product to making another similar product. During set-up time the machinery is idle and non-productive while all the other operating expenses continue. If the downtime is too long or happens too often, the company will be hurt financially. Larger customers may demand that long production runs, which keep costs down, be interrupted to fill immediate needs for specific products.

On the other hand, when the manufacturer sells through a wholesale distributor, the distributor's inventory should serve the needs of the customer between the time the manufacturer's inventories are depleted and the next production run is started. The distributor's inventories will also help buffer any large surges in sales which might occur. An early order entered by a distributor signals the manufacturer that the needs of the marketplace are changing, allowing it to adjust its production schedules to meet the new demands. These surges in sales are easily detected by manufacturers who market through distributors who, via bar code scanners, capture the sale of all products daily and make this information available to their manufacturers through computer networks.

Local inventory is essential if customers are to receive products at a high service level. If distributors did not purchase and provide that local inventory, the manufacturer would have to build or rent warehouse space and stock it with merchandise. This would further extend the cash flow, raise the cost of storage and increase the cost of goods to the consumers. The cost of storage would be increased because only one product line would have to absorb the total expense of warehousing. In the wholesale distributorship, this cost is spread over many product lines.

According to research done by the American Supply and Machinery Manufacturers Association (ASMMA), just over one-half of the industrial goods which are sold through distributors are sold in only 50 major market areas in the United States. Imagine the expense of a manufacturer operating 50 warehousing operations in 50 major cities from coast to coast! Using the distributor's warehouse facilities is much more economical.

Another function the wholesale distributor provides the manufacturer is the local transportation of products to the end users. This eliminates purchase or rental of 50 fleets of trucks. Of course, trucks must be provided by the distributor or another service provider. However, the cost of transportation is spread over all of the products the distributor is delivering and not borne by a single manufacturer.

The wholesale distributor performs marketplace functions for both manufacturers and customers. Keep in mind that the selling strength and operating efficiencies of the distributor are the greatest asset to the manufacturer, while the distributors buying strength and ability to spread the operating cost over many customers is the greatest asset for the contractor and industrial user. Because competition is keen and distributors are highly motivated, these functions are performed for a modest (if not meager) profit.

Nine

Investment And Risk

You may have heard the cliche, "It takes money to make money." Did you ever stop to consider where the original investment money comes from? It comes from savings which can be generated by individuals or companies. People who work for wages, but are conservative, may save enough money from their pay check to eventually become self-employed. This was the case of Andrew Carnegie. He started working for wages as a young Scottish immigrant. He saved as much as he could from his job as a telegraph operator working for the Pennsylvania Railroad. He was a bright and energetic person, and after being promoted to superintendent developed the Pullman sleeping car. He later resigned to start his own company, the Keystone Bridge Company. He and his associates built the company into a giant. Carnegie later sold out to J. P. Morgan's steel company for $250 million and became a devoted philanthropist. None of this would have been possible without enough savings to get started.

Corporations also save when they can. Like Carnegie, their savings are usually reinvested back into the company. However, like the workers who spend most of their money for food, clothing, housing and transportation before they can save, corporations spend most of their income for raw materials, inventory, tools, marketing expenses, wages and benefits, taxes and payments to stockholders. This leaves only a small percentage which can be saved or reinvested in the company.

Business is the source of most of our savings. The business which makes a product efficiently or provides a service which fulfills a need has an opportunity to save a small amount after expenses. However, if employees demand too great an increase in wages or benefits, customers demand that the line be held on prices, if the government taxes the individuals or corporation excessively for welfare benefits or other non-productive spending programs, then the company will have no savings and thus no money to reinvest in new products or machinery to create new jobs.

Even if the government used the tax money collected from individuals and corporations to create jobs within the government, most of the money for the salaries of the new job holders still must come from business. As badly as we need public employees such as teachers, firemen, policemen and other city, county and federal employees, they generate no new revenue. Yes, they pay taxes but do not produce new revenues. New revenues come from business.

Assuming that a small portion of money remains after expenses and wages have been paid by a company, we can call this savings, or more appropriately, "profit." For the wholesale distributor, profit after tax on income from sales or services is about two dollars of every $100 of income. The other $98 goes to pay suppliers of products for the inventory, to provide storage, equipment and fork lifts, to pay employee wages and benefits, and to pay local, state, and federal taxes. The money that remains (profits) is usually divided into shareholders dividends and reinvestment funds. The reinvestment funds (profits) are utilized to purchase new product lines, improve customer services or increase inventories and accounts receivable, and thus stabilize existing jobs and create new ones. There is no job security in any industry which does not generate a reasonable profit.

A point of clarification is important here. <u>The free enterprise system is not a "profit system" but a "profit or loss system.</u>" A company which is well managed and not over-taxed can and should generate a reasonable profit. Success for a wholesale distributor is measured by that exact method. How much profit did the company make with the funds they had invested? However, not all companies can generate profits and some, therefore, have extensive losses and eventually fail.

A simple measure of the investment in a distributorship is this: if the management had chosen not to invest in the company but had put its money in a savings account, it would have received interest for the deposit. Interest on a savings account is like profit. To stockholders who invest in a company, the profit which is divided among them is called dividends. To a company which reinvests in itself, it is called retained earnings or profit. Regardless of what it is called, profit, in this case, is a measure of money made with money.

The wholesale distributor invests money in inventory, accounts receivable, buildings, salaries and benefits for employees. Inventories of 200 to 50,000 different items, ranging in value from $100,000 to $100 million, are commonplace. A rule of thumb is that the average wholesale distributor will have one person on the payroll for every $400,000 to $800,000 in sales, depending upon the efficiency of the operation and the products being handled. The higher the sales volume the more job opportunities will be available with that firm.

The cost of the inventory and accounts receivable are major expense items for the distributor and weigh heavily on the profit determination. The distributor's service is dependent upon having sufficient inventory to fulfill customers' needs, without having too much. The money to purchase additional merchandise to be put into inventory for resale comes from after tax savings or profits.

In order to better understand the cost-profit relationship, several basic terms will be discussed. The cost of the merchandise is a commonly used term known as the "Cost of Goods Sold" (COGS).

Cost of Merchandise + Freight = COGS

If a wholesale distributor sold an item to a customer for $100, roughly $75 to $80 would go to cover the cost of the goods sold (COGS).

The $20 to $25 which remained would be called the gross margin. The difference between the price the customer pays for the merchandise and the COGS is the gross margin. If the term "selling price" is used to indicate the actual price paid by the customer, then the selling price minus the COGS is equal to the gross margin.

Selling Price (actual amount received) - COGS = Gross Margin

In order for a distributor to stay in business and offer jobs for employees, sufficient gross margin must be generated to cover the expenses of purchasing inventory, selling, warehousing, extending credit, keeping records, paying employee wages and benefits, providing transportation, and paying administrative costs, utilities, taxes, interest of borrowed money, and profit (or savings).

A rule of thumb is that 30-60 percent of the gross margin will be used to pay employee wages and benefits. In the example of the $100 sale, $80 was spent for COGS. Twenty dollars remained as gross margin, one-half of which ($10) went to the distributor's employees for wages and benefits. Few employees really understand the significance of the expense their employers incur in providing benefits such as social security, worker's compensation insurance, paid vacations, paid holidays, retirement benefits, supplemental insurance premiums, and other benefits.

It is natural that employees relate primarily to the net amount of their payroll check after all of the deductions have been removed, because this is the amount which can be spent for the necessities of life. However, the employer is spending a great deal more than even the gross amount shown on the face of the check. Responsible employees will realize and appreciate the total contribution of the distributor to their overall financial well being. Since employee wages and benefits consume roughly half of the gross margin which is available from sales, it is the distributor's single greatest expense. However, people are the distributor's single greatest asset. Every successful distributor has developed quality personnel who are dedicated to the purposes of the company, give more than is expected, and believe in the free enterprise system. These same distributors expect a great deal from employees, but reward them openly for jobs well done. People are the key to any wholesale distributor operation and make substantial contributions to profits.

The other expense categories which are paid from the gross margin dollars are physical facilities, transportation equipment, machinery, utilities, interest, and taxes which consume from $7 to $8 of the remaining $10. The $2 which remain from the $100 sale, after expenses, can be saved (or reinvested) and is called profit. Two percent is a meager profit indeed. Even so, the successful distributor who turns (buys and sells) the inventory five consecutive times in one year can make a reasonable profit. Although it may not provide an excellent return, considering the risks involved, most distributors view it as sufficient to warrant their continuation in the business.

The Financial Risk

The distributor management purchases inventory which they plan to sell to contractors or industrial consumers in their marketing areas. The wise distributor does not plan to "sell what is in inventory," but purchases and markets "what the customers need" and will purchase. The difference in the two concepts weighs heavily on the financial risk involved. Few distributors are willing to invest in exotic items which might sell "some day" even if the potential profits are high. Most wholesale distributors are deeply involved in providing a service to customers by having what their customers need at the time it is needed. This not only increases the service factor, it reduces the risk. Unfortunately, economic reversals, such as recessions, do occur; they are a risk to the distributor and can and often do cause financial losses. Many times recessions do not simply occur. They are planned to cool inflation.

One means of controlling (cooling) inflation is for the Federal government to restrict the amount of money available. When money is in short supply, interest rates for borrowed monies are raised. The rise in interest rates makes goods and services more expensive so consumers cut back on credit purchases and recession (a down-turn in business) follows.

During recessions, profits fall for most distributors. Many have experienced financial losses during recent recessions because of lost sales. As interest rates for manufactured housing (mobile homes) and single family residential dwellings increase, consumers can no longer afford the house payments and refuse to buy. Building materials distributors who had not anticipated the down-turn and reduced their inventories accordingly were hard pressed financially when sales declined. Since some part of the American economy, or one or more geographic regions, has experienced a recession every three to five years since 1950, the threat of economic loss is always present--thus the profit or loss system.

Recession is not the only factor in considering economic loss. The closing of the facility of a major customer or government agency, the bankruptcy of a major contractor who owed the distributor money, poor management, labor problems, high interest rates on borrowed money, the loss of a major product line, and many other elements can cause a distributor to take a financial loss.

The point of the discussion is this: the distributor takes a financial risk because inventory is purchased on the presumption that it can be sold at a profit. The availability of the product in the local market provides a service for the customers. The willingness of the wholesale distributor to assume the risk of losing money, while being of service, warrants the right of the well managed company to expect to earn a reasonable profit.

To some business managers, the idea of earning a profit means that at the end of the year profit is what is left over (remains after all bills and taxes are paid). However, this method of operation is not the design of dynamic business people.

Distributor management which views profit as "what remains after all expenses have been paid" is not progressive. In fact profit should be planned, projected, and "taken off the top." This may be a new concept for many but not for those managers who have always projected sales, gross margins, expenses, and profits. If the sales projections are correct, gross margins are achieved as expected, then profit can and should be "taken off the top." How? By controlling the only remaining variable, "allowable expenses." They are not called expenses but allowable expense because people both make money and spend money. Every time money is spent, someone made the decision to spend it. If the decisions to spend are within the allowable expense properly planned for that sale, then the subsequent portions of the gross margin from that sale are profit.

However, if an extended hour of overtime is worked by an hourly employee, an extra long distance call is made, the merchandise is returned by the customer, a customer fails to pay receivables on time, or any other thing which increases allowable expenses, then the profit is reduced by that same amount.

The relationship between costs and profits is inversely proportional. As costs go up $1, profits go down $1. Only about two percent of the total sale price is profit and only then if the line is held on allowable expenses. You, as an employee, must be a contributing factor to the profit of your company and should support the profit motive whenever you hear it being discussed. The job you enjoy depends on it.

Some types of sales are more profitable than others. The controversial issue of the profitability of drop shipments will be discussed next.

Ten

Direct Shipments and Their Profitability

A common type of sale in the industrial construction business is the direct or "drop" shipment. This occurs when the distributor takes an order (usually for a larger-than-ordinary volume of goods) and rather than pulling the merchandise from local inventory, arranges to have the manufacturer ship the goods directly to the customer. Many contractors expect this type of service for their larger construction projects in order to successfully compete for construction contracts.

The use of direct shipments in some cases seems to hold some advantages for both the distributor and the customer. For instance, delivery costs are typically paid by the manufacturer and the distributor incurs no material-handling expenses. The inventory carrying costs associated with warehousing enough stock to fill large orders such as stocking activities, insurance, pilferage, damage during handling, etc., are eliminated because the goods do not pass through the distributor's warehouse.

This cost reduction can allow the distributor to sell the goods at a lower gross margin percentage while still retaining a marginal profit. These legitimate cost savings may be passed on to the customer. However, the question is: <u>Just how much of a savings does the distributor actually realize in these cases and what should the gross margin percentage be on direct shipments</u>?

After consulting with a random sample of wholesale distributors, the information gathered suggests that many of these sales are not as profitable as many distributors believe.

Pure Profit?

While the author recognizes that most distributors prefer to sell out of stock, direct shipments are a fact of life in the industry and are tolerated because of their perceived "easy profitability." Some even suggested that "someone is going to take the business, and two percent of something is better than 100 percent of nothing." Others stringently disagree because they know that to sell at two percent is to sell at a loss.

Even so, most of the distributors interviewed consider a direct-shipment order a "no-cost" sale. They did not believe significant operating costs were involved and contended that the margin made was pure profit. For instance, one distributor argued that because the salespeople were on salary, they were going to be paid whether or not any orders for direct shipments were taken.

This kind of thinking will erode a distributor's profits quickly. Salespeople are hired to make sales in the best interests of the company, while meeting the customer's needs, including direct shipments. If a salesperson is paid on commission, then there is certainly a selling expense associated with any direct sale made. If not, the salesperson has spent time with a customer taking an order for the direct shipment and may have lost an opportunity to make a warehouse sale at a higher margin. So, a "lost opportunity cost" is involved.

Another issue is the time required for a salesperson to work up a bid and to submit it for a direct-shipment sale. Key indications show that even more time may be required than for a regular sale. If the sale is made on the salesperson's time, it's costing the distributor money.

Other cost factors beyond selling expenses that must be considered include general and administrative (G&A) costs, as well as the expenses to occupy the building (rent, electricity, etc.). In addition, a salaried person processes the order, arranges for shipment with the manufacturer, and follows up on it in the same manner as for a warehouse sale. In some companies there is additional work involved in processing these orders for direct shipments. There may also be risks incurred due to high credit exposure of large dollar orders, as well as decreased inventory turns.

Very few of the companies interviewed calculated these costs and passed them along to the customers. All activities undertaken by distributor employees in support of a direct shipment sale must be accounted for in the gross margin if the direct shipment sale is to be profitable. This can be accomplished by conducting an activity based costing study where every single activity is listed and cost determined.

Another argument presented in justification of low gross margins was that direct shipments are such a small percentage of business that they do not affect bottom-line profits. This may be true for some distributors, but others produce a much larger percentage of their sales volume by direct shipment.

According to a recent <u>Industry Performance Survey</u> published by the National Association of Wholesale Distributors, wholesale distributors with sales between $3 million and $12 million handled, on average, close to 20 percent of their business on a direct-shipment basis. Can distributors afford to break even or possibly lose money on 20 percent of their sales? None of the distributors who supplied information for this study believe they can.

Fewer Resources, But They Cost Money

Every sale that a company makes requires resources to support the selling activity. These resources are staff and other company assets (primarily receivables in this case) that are used to conduct day-to-day business. Obviously, a direct shipment requires the use of fewer support resources. However, some companies believe that direct shipments represent "extra" or "plus business" and are unbudgeted sales that can fit into the "system" because generally any system is operating below capacity. When viewed from this perspective, a direct shipment would appear to have fewer costs associated with it because under-utilized resources are being used to process the sale.

The critical issue becomes: <u>Did your company budget for the sale</u>? Or, is it truly extra business that will simply bring operations closer to capacity?

If the company budget includes such activities (as most do to some extent), it is likely that <u>resources have already been allocated</u> to support them. Fewer resources may be needed for this sale; nonetheless, these resources have definite costs associated with them and must be charged against that sale in order to evaluate the true level of profitability. For instance, if 10 percent of your budget is allocated to support direct shipments, this 10 percent must be charged against these sales before any profit from that sale can be assumed. All over ten percent may be extra business, but the first 10 percent is not.

You can break these operating expenses into six categories: selling, delivery, warehouse, general and administrative (G&A), interest on borrowed monies and occupancy. Clearly, delivery and warehouse expenses will not be incurred on a direct shipment sale. But what about selling, G&A and occupancy expenses? Let's take a look.

Selling Expenses: Selling costs can be defined as those associated with maintaining a sales force. The salaries of clerical and secretarial personnel who support the selling activity are also included, in addition to the costs for compiling bids for direct-shipment sales. Clearly, if a direct shipment sale is to be evaluated on a stand-alone basis in terms of its effect on profitability, this selling expense must be charged against the sale. The consensus among the distributors contacted was that direct sales took as much and, in some cases, more time to handle as a comparably-sized stock sale.

General and Administrative (G&A) Expenses: G&A includes such items as executive and management salaries and bonuses, as well as many other costs that do not fit into any other category. Since these expenses are of a general nature, it is easy to assume they are fixed costs and are incurred whether or not direct shipment sales are made. If this is the case, general and administrative expenses should not be charged against a direct-shipment sale.

However, there are a number of expenses that are included in G&A that relate to direct-shipment sales: purchasing, stationery and printing, telephone, postage, collection, bad debt and accounting services. All will rise directly with increases in direct-shipment sales and the size of the orders and should be charged against them.

Given the number of expense categories included in G&A and the number of categories that increase with an increase in direct-shipment sales, this percentage normally falls between 15 percent and 20 percent.

Again, the critical issue with G&A expense is whether or not the company has budgeted for direct-shipment sales. If it has, then it is likely that support resources have been allocated. In that case, a higher percentage of G&A expense should be used in evaluating the profitability of these sales. In addition, sometimes this takes a large portion of the owner/manager's time which might have been better utilized in evaluating new high margin lines or working on improving the process of company operations so that continuous improvement in quality and customer satisfaction could be achieved.

Occupancy Expenses: These probably do not automatically increase with direct-shipment sales. It is easy to see that a firm will incur the costs of occupying a building and related maintenance expenses whether or not direct-shipment sales are made.

Money-Losing Proposition?

As already noted, for a firm with $3 million to $12 million in annual sales volume, the Industry Performance Survey reports that, on average, 20 percent of those sales are direct or drop shipments. The gross margin on those sales averaged 11.71 percent, ranging from an approximate low of 9.84 percent to an approximate high of 13.5 percent. If two other costs — the typical selling expense of 7 percent and the aforementioned 20 percent of the reported G&A expense — are factored into the cost of making such sales, then it may be concluded that only a small percentage of profit can be attributed to direct shipments. (See Exhibit 1.)

Exhibit 1:

Average Gross Margin on Direct Sales		11.71%
Less Related Operating Expense		
Selling Expense	7.0%	
G&A Expense	1.77%	8.77%
Profit Before Interest and Taxes		2.94%

If the gross margin from the lower end of the range of margins reported is used, then the profitability looks even worse. The associated expenses decline, but so does the profit associated with the direct-shipment sales for these lower-margin firms. Exhibit 2 shows these results.

Exhibit 2:

Gross Margin on Direct Sales		9.84%
Less Related Operating Expenses		
Selling Expense	6.67%	
G&A Expense	1.69%	8.36%
Profit Before Interest and Taxes		1.48%

It would appear that wholesale distributors are experiencing only marginal profitability on their direct-shipment sales when all of the costs related to these sales are taken into consideration. It is easy to see that only a small pricing mistake could turn a sale with these low margins into a money-losing proposition.

Another consideration is the gross margins used in constructing both exhibits. Some of the suppliers who were interviewed indicated that five percent or less was an adequate gross margin on a large direct shipment because the larger the direct order, the lower the cost as a percent of the sale. While this is true, what cost is associated with the additional credit risk of the larger order? In any event, reducing the margins used in our examples to five percent would result in a net loss in both cases.

Even with these facts on hand, some distributors will still take an occasional drop shipment for the two percent cash discount. In light of the above facts, they may be selling themselves out of business without even knowing it.

Beware of Extending Cash Discounts

Another cost that must be considered is associated with the credit a distributor extends to the buyer between the time the distributor's firm pays for the merchandise and the time it receives payment from the buyer. Included would be a discount that may be offered for prompt payment.

Some of the suppliers interviewed offer such a discount for direct-shipment invoices just as they do for stock sales. These payment terms were usually 2/10, net/30, although in a few cases they were 2/10, net/11. Some were cash on delivery.

Others, however, did not offer discounts on direct shipments. They recognized that these sales were indeed different from warehouse sales in that they were made at much lower gross margins. In most cases, these suppliers requested payment of direct-shipment invoices in ten days.

To illustrate the impact on profitability of extending credit to buyers and offering discounts for early payment, let us examine a hypothetical direct-shipment transaction that involved merchandise costing your firm $20,408.

Consider the following example:

— No cash discount is offered on the sale and the customer remits payment to the distributor on the 30th day after invoicing.
— Your firm has a standing policy of taking all cash discounts, so you remit to the manufacturer a payment of $20,000 ($20,408 - 2% = $20,000) on the tenth day after the merchandise was delivered to your customer.

Your selling price is calculated using your cost after the cash discount and the average gross margin of 11.71 percent. Your invoice price to the customer is $22,653 ($20,000/.8829 = $22,653).

Since you did not pay the manufacturer for ten days and your customer did not pay you for 30 days after receiving the merchandise, in effect you have extended credit to your customer in the amount of $22,653 for 20 days. The cost of extending this credit is the interest you could have earned on the outstanding amount at the going rate for 20 days. It will be assumed that the money could have been invested at nine percent annual rate for 20 days. The following calculation shows the cost per day of "loaning" your customer $22,653 at nine percent interest:

$$\frac{\$22,653 \times .09}{365} = \$5.59 \text{ per day}$$

The cost of extending this credit to your customer for the 20-day period is $5.59 per day x 20 days = $111.80.

Exhibit 3 illustrates the stand-alone profitability of this direct sale, using the expense percentages developed in Exhibit 1.

Exhibit 3:

Drop Shipment at 11.71% Gross Margin

Revenue from Direct Sale	$22,653		100.0%
Cost of Goods Sold	<20,000>		88.29
Gross Margin	2,653		11.71
Operating Expenses			
Selling Expense	<$1,586>	7.00%	
G&A Expense	<401>	1.77	
		8.77	<8.77>
Operating Profit	$666		2.94
Cost of Extending Credit	<112>		<0.5%>
Profit Before Tax	$544		2.44%

If the gross margin experienced by the lower-margin companies and the related expenses as illustrated in Exhibit 3 are used in examining the profitability of this direct sale, the dollar profit becomes meager indeed.

Exhibit 4:

Drop Shipment at 9.84% Gross Margin

Revenue from Direct Sale	$22,183	100.0%
Cost of Goods Sold	<20,000>	<90.16>
Gross Margin	2,183	9.84
Operating Expense		
Selling Expense	<$1,480>	6.67%
G&A Expense	< 375>	1.69
		8.36 <8.36>
Operating Profit	$ 328	1.48
Cost of Extending Credit	<110>	<0.50>
Profit Before Tax	$ 218	.98

    Again, if the gross margin on these sales was reduced to five percent or less, as is a common practice in some industries, both of these last two examples would show net losses.

    If your firm offers a cash discount on direct-shipment sales, the bottom-line profitability associated with those sales will be lower than those shown in Exhibits 3 and 4. While the costs of extending credit to the customer will be reduced, the reduction in price offered for prompt payment more than offsets this reduction in "credit" costs.

Using the example in Exhibit 3, which prices the sale to yield an 11.71 percent gross margin, Exhibit 5 shows the effect of a one percent cash discount for payment within 10 days. Notice that there is no cost of extending credit in this example. That's because it is assumed that your customers pay you on the tenth day after receiving the invoice — the same day on which you pay the manufacturer for the goods.

Exhibit 5:

Drop Shipment at 11.71% Gross Margin, with 1% Cash Discount

Revenue from Direct Sale	53	100.0%
Less: Purchase Discount	1>	1.0
Net Revenue from Direct Sale	22,426	99.0
Cost of Goods Sold	<20,000>	88.29
Gross Margin	2,426	10.71
Operating Expense		
Selling Expense	$1,586 7.0%	
G&A Expense	401 1.77	
Total Expenses	1,987 8.77	8.77%
Profit Before Tax	$439	1.94%

Exhibit 6 does not include any cost of extending credit because it is assumed your customer pays you on the same day on which you pay the manufacturer, the tenth day.

Exhibit 6:

Drop Shipment at 11.71% Gross margin, with 2% Cash Discount

Revenue from Direct Sale	$22,653	100.0%
Less: Purchase Discount	<453>	2.0
Net Revenue from Direct Sale	22,200	98.0
Cost of Goods Sold	<20,000>	88.29
Gross Margin	2,200	9.71
Operating Expense		
Selling Expense	$1,586	7.0%
G&A Expense	401	1.77
Total Expenses	1,987 8.77	8.77%
Profit Before Tax	$213	0.94%

What About The Intangibles?

Many of the distributors the author studied believed that the lower margins on direct shipments were justifiable because of the intangible benefits received from providing this service. An intangible benefit is one that occurs because of a given sale but cannot always be tied directly to that sale.

A good example is an add-on sale. Many large construction jobs handled by contractors receive the majority of goods by direct shipment. However, the contractor may require additional or fill-in supplies as the job continues. The customer who prefers to work with only one supplier may return to that company for the extra materials needed. Purchased from stock, these materials will likely carry a higher margin than direct-shipment goods. Although the actual profit from these add-on sales would not be shown with the initial order, they may be considered an intangible (non-accountable) benefit of the direct-shipment sales.

Goodwill is an even less tangible by-product of the direct-shipment process. Because direct shipments are usually for large-volume sales, some of the companies interviewed arranged them in order to provide customers with a better price. This may enhance goodwill and plant the seeds for a relationship that will lead to future sales, but these future sales may be at significantly lower margins because of the prices established for the drop shipment. Most of the high-profit distributors believe that in today's market there is no allegiance or loyalty anymore, and that "goodwill is a fantasy."

Some companies even have salespeople who follow-up the direct-shipment sale to make sure that everything arrives in order and the customer is satisfied. This is often necessary because the distributor has no control over the manufacturer's shipments. This extra effort actually costs the company additional time and expense, and may or may not bring additional future business.

While these intangible benefits may be real, are they reason enough to justify low margins on direct-shipment sales?

The more profitable distributors said no — not at the expense of profit. There are too many risks in depending on these benefits that may cause an unprofitable sale.

The biggest risk can come from offering a low margin. Many customers do not understand that the relatively low cost of a direct shipment is due to decreased expenses incurred by the distributor. Consequently, they may come to expect the same low prices when they purchase material from the distributor's stock. Distributors must realize that offering such low prices may be giving a customer valuable price information that could work against them (particularly if the distributor marks them up five percent or less).

Depending on future or add-on sales to make direct shipments profitable can be dangerous. In today's highly competitive market, too many customers are simply looking for the lowest price on every single transaction and will cherry-pick your bid when allowed to, and thus do not offer the kind of long-term relationship the distributor had anticipated when the direct shipment was arranged. Quoting a low price once to get a customer locked into your company will give that customer the wrong impression about the way you handle business. It could lead to the customer's disappointment with your company later.

Conclusion

Use activity based costing to calculate the exact and complete cost for your firm to take a drop-shipment order. Do not make assumptions you should not make. Add up all the costs. Do not sell below your required net profit before tax. Make every sale profitable on its own merit. There is always business that you cannot afford to take.

Some of the business distributors cannot afford to take are those sales in which products are returned. In some cases as much as ten percent of the material purchased for a construction job will be requested to be returned to the distributor at the close of the project, even though much of it was drop shipped. This is very costly to both the distributor and the customer and must be dealt with openly.

Eleven

The Cost Of Quality Versus Returned Goods

Many large customers of wholesale distributors have implemented the total quality process which is designed to bring about continuous improvements in the quality of their goods and services. This in turn will improve customer satisfaction with their products, as well as cut their costs because they did it right the first time. Continuous improvement is meant to insure that they will remain competitive into the future.

As a result, these customers are identifying what it costs them when the distributor makes a mistake in inside sales, order entry, pricing, purchasing, accounting, billing, picking, packing or shipping to them. These errors cost them from $50 to $100 each in reprocessing expenses and follow-up, not to mention possible down-time in the plant. Most of these companies are quickly reaching the point at which they will no longer tolerate back orders, shipments that are wrong, short, long, late or early, or other mistakes distributors make because of the costs and hassle involved.

Because of this, these customers are reducing the number of distributors and manufacturers from which they purchase original equipment and maintenance supplies by 80 percent or more. One of the methods used to determine those vendors that will keep the accounts will be the number of errors made by each in 25 different categories. The customer will determine the category, and in the beginning will keep records on how well the vendors perform in the area being measured.

Where customers have accepted two errors per 100 lines of billing in the past, some are now demanding only one or two errors in 1,000 lines of billing, or less. The quality process calls for continuous improvement so even this small number of errors will not be sufficient for an extended period of time. The goal is zero errors and even beyond. Going beyond zero errors means that we must not only make no errors, but must anticipate what the customer will need even before the need is known and have the product or service available before it is requested.

Wholesale distributors contend daily with the problem of errors and thus returned goods. Few days pass without at least one customer wanting to return a previously purchased item for credit or exchange. The return could be for any number of reasons: the item was shipped wrong, ordered wrong, or damaged when received, or the customer simply didn't need the item when it arrived. The question for suppliers is not whether the return should be honored. In a service-oriented business, your customer's needs must be addressed courteously. The question is how much does it cost the distributor to receive a returned good and how do you reduce the returns and their costs.

In times of ever-increasing competition, higher costs of money, lower productivity, and the threat of vendor reduction, the distributor must review all errors and their costs carefully and minimize them to keep the business profitable. The cost of returned goods is no exception.

Most distributors have not been too concerned with this cost. Typically, they said, "It is only two percent of our business and therefore is not significant," or they said, "We have a restocking charge to compensate us." But they must ask themselves: Does that charge fully cover the costs of accepting the returned goods? A research study by Dr. Madelaine Lowe at Texas A&M University says no. The study, based upon the operations of several large supply houses, indicates that the thought that a restocking charge can cover the cost of handling a returned item stems from a terrible misunderstanding by many owners, managers and employees of wholesale distributorships.

For example, if a distributor charges a 15 percent restocking charge on a $10 item, the charge would be only $1.50; on a $100 item, it would be $15. The problem, of course, is that the time and other costs of handling a returned item do not vary directly with its price. Taking back a $10 item costs as much as taking back a $100 item because the paperwork and restocking are about the same. Whether you are fully compensated depends on the price of the item returned and whether or not you can or will charge all of your customers.

Using a percentage-based charge also creates a problem when the item has such a high price that the restocking charge seems too high to justify. Suppose a customer walks in to return a $150 hydraulic pump. Most distributors would not be inclined to charge $22.50 (15 percent of $150) for restocking. They often reduce or waive the charge. In this example, the distributor loses money by reducing the $22.50 charge at all.

According to the study mentioned above, each stock item returned costs from $30 to $60, plus the cost of employee benefits. With a 15 percent restocking charge, the minimum dollar value of the returned item would have to be about $200 just to break even. With this knowledge, it's easy to see what a $10 return with a 15 percent restocking charge will net.

$30.00	Cost to accept return
− 1.50	Restocking Charge
$28.50	Loss

It is not suggested that the distributor charge $28.50 for all returns. No one would pay this flat rate to return a $10, $30 or even $50 item. But knowing this cost and where it is incurred may help employees understand the need to reduce it. Keep in mind that these errors also cost the customer from $50 to $100 each time they occur.

The returned goods process also has some important hidden costs that could not be accounted for in the $30-$60. Two hidden costs relate to what happens to the inventory while the customer has the item. First, the inventory is reduced.

Because the item is unavailable in inventory, its absence could cause a shortage that keeps the distributor from getting a potential sale—perhaps even a customer. Second, the distributor may order more of the item to restock inventory. After the item is returned, the distributor is over-stocked on the item and has money tied up in excess inventory of that item. These hidden costs are two more reasons to implement the quality process, which is designed to eliminate the errors caused by your current faulty process.

Most distributors simply don't know what it costs their companies to handle returned goods, nor do they equate the expense to the dollars in sales required to support it. Look at the dollars of sales required, using the net profit before taxes (NPBT) to sales as generally earned by wholesale distributors.

A distributor with six returns per day, which were caused by his errors, at $30 each, needs $9,000 in sales each working day to support six unnecessary returns: 6 x $30 = $180 per day, which was the NPBT that was eroded by the cost of handling the returns. Divide $180 by .02, (two percent NPBT) and you get $9,000 of sales needed to generate $180 NPBT, which was spent to cover the cost of unnecessary errors.

If that same distributor could reduce average returns from six to five per day, the dollars in sales needed to support this cost would drop from about $9,000 to about $7,500. The distributor should not overlook the big potential savings.

Respondents to the research study also typically said, "Our returns are handled by regular employees and therefore are part of our fixed costs." They are right, but fixed costs erode profitability as do variable costs. Excesses in fixed costs are just harder to spot. Therefore, the distributor should look closely at how many returns the company gets each month. Finding the cause may help you identify means of changing the system so that the errors can be eliminated, not identified after the fact. A carefully drawn flow chart of the work in progress and a cross-sectional cost analysis will be required for you to see how the process really works as opposed to how you think it works.

Some of the statements heard during the interviews at wholesale distributorships showed a major lack of understanding of the costs of handling returns. Some employees even encouraged returns. For example, one conversation at a city counter went like this: (Customer) "I'm not sure whether that conduit was three-quarters of an inch or one inch." (Salesperson) "Well, go ahead and take both fittings and just bring whichever size you don't need back for credit." The salesperson is just creating more work, and realizing it or not, is probably eliminating the profit on $30 divided by .02, or $1,500 in sales. Remember that the cost/profit relationship is a one-to-one ratio and is inversely proportional for both the wholesale distributor and the customer. Every dollar in costs erodes a dollar in NPBT. Because time is money, minimize the time spent on unnecessary returns so that employees can use their time to make profits.

The Cross-Sectional Cost Analysis

To develop a way to measure the cost of handling returned goods, first establish a list of functions performed during the return process. This can best be performed by drawing a process flow diagram which depicts each step in the returned goods process. To do just that, Dr. Madelaine Lowe extensively studied three large industrial distributors in the South. She developed a returned goods checklist that identifies and explains 42 functions in the return process. The modified checklist, displayed at the end of this chapter, was later used in a study of electrical distributorships to determine the $27.47 average cost of handling returned goods shown in the table. In researching each category on the checklist, the researchers extensively interviewed each person doing the various tasks to determine an average time per function. Branch managers provided an average pay scale for the person doing the work in the non-union companies (time allotments and pay rates may differ). The minutes required for each task then were multiplied by the appropriate wage to get the cost of each function. Costs of employee benefits, including Social Security, workman's compensation insurance, vacations and other employee benefits, were not added. In this respect, the costs for your company may be significantly higher than stated here.

The total cost for a returned item naturally differs according to how it must be handled and how much time it requires. For example, a non-stock item, which must be returned to the vendor, will cost more than a stock return because of the time needed to call the vendor for return authorization, arrange and pay freight for the return, follow up on these arrangements, and perhaps pay a restocking charge by the factory. None of these activities is required when a stock item is returned to the distributor's inventory. In fact, many situations could call for unusual activities. An example would be damaged-goods claims with freight companies. Because the study could not address all possibilities, it calculated only the two most common problems: stock items and non-stock items.

The average cost to the electrical distributorship for a stock-item return was calculated to be $27.47. This cost included transportation, checking, restocking, issuing credit, and handling all paperwork and administration. It did not include picking, packing and shipping the right product or a replacement, nor did it consider a restocking charge. To determine the out-of-pocket costs with restocking charge, simply subtract the funds received from the returned goods charge from the average cost to handle the return.

The other category measured, non-stock returns, was found to cost considerably more at $43.39 per line of billing. This estimate assumes, of course, that the distributor passes on to the customer any restocking charges imposed by the manufacturer. In addition to the time spent arranging to return the item to the vendor, the biggest part of the cost was the freight, which averaged $12.10. Manufacturers do not seem to mind charging their "good" customers restocking expenses. Maybe distributors should take lessons.

Visible Costs Per Returned Good

The visible or known cost for each return was $27.47 for stock and $43.39 for non-stock returns. For general line distributors the cost was $30 to $60. For the customer the cost is also from $40 to $60. Any distributor can gather this same information by making a simple function-time checklist. Check the items in the form provided that apply to your company's returned goods procedure (add other items as needed), and assign the time in minutes and the cost of the time to each activity. With this information, calculate what it really costs the company to handle a return.

To pinpoint excess costs of returned goods and other errors, review the number of credit memos processed and tally the reasons for the errors. This should uncover problems with customers that can and must be solved. The researchers pulled the credit memos issued from a large branch during two months to determine how many returns had been received and what the major reasons were. Their findings show that 104 credit memos were processed for an average of two returns per day (104 memos divided by 50 working days in two months is two per day). But the memos do not reflect all returns handled during those two months. According to the outside salespeople, an average of one return or exchange per day never went through the paperwork route. With these returns, the customer is billed correctly for an item but is either shipped the wrong item or is shorted. These situations don't call for paperwork changes. But the salespeople spend time exchanging the item on their regular calls, or they have a company truck pick up the item on the next delivery. These returns may not cost much in paperwork, but they are expensive because of lost selling time by salespeople and lost goodwill with customers. These errors must not be ignored: They cost!

The research also found that 44 percent of these returns had been shipped as ordered. This finding indicated that the items were returned because the customer either ordered incorrectly or simply refused the goods. Only 30 percent of these returns were charged for restocking, although the company had a policy of charging 25 percent for all returns that were not its fault. Of the 30 percent charged, all but two were assessed only 15 percent.

The two most common reasons given for not following the policy were 1) "We don't charge our good customers" and 2) "The policy is used only to discourage returns, and we don't enforce it unless our manufacturer charges us for restocking." Both reasons suggest a lack of managerial communication about company policy and little concern by anyone about the cost of returns. The company thus loses money and does not deter customers from frequently returning goods. Of course, the real answer is to do it right the first time so that the customer is made happy and does not return the goods.

Find the Problems

After the cost of returned goods has been determined, and the most common reasons for them are known, the distributor can identify the most prevalent and expensive problems. You can then whittle away those problems and reduce the costs. You must stop treating the symptoms and start treating the causes. Instead of accepting so many returned goods, slow them or stop them. Learn why goods are coming back and who caused the unsatisfactory shipment. Find the mistakes and correct the cause. This can only be accomplished by implementing the total quality process. Dr. W. Edwards Deming, the father of the quality process, indicates that 85 percent of all of the problems in industry are caused by a faulty system, while only 15 percent are caused by the people working in the system. Therefore, it behooves the distributor management to learn the quality process and spend its time changing the system so errors can be prevented, not corrected.

Many problems are preventable. For example, 29 percent of the returns were for cost adjustments. Are distributors spending enough time with inside salespeople and pricing clerks, providing them with pricing information satisfactory to the customers? Current data implies that proper training requires that the distributor spend from three to seven percent of payroll on training. Are you even close?

Another 14 percent of the merchandise was returned because it was damaged. Are people checking the merchandise? Are they handling it carelessly? Try to learn why an item was damaged and by whom. What is it about your system that allows this to happen? Is your order picking route system arranged so that heavy materials are picked last and are being thrown on top of lighter materials picked earlier? This may be both a system and a personnel training problem, but it certainly can be solved.

Another 9 percent was returned because of an error in shipping. The item was either duplicated or over-shipped, or the wrong one was sent. Why was the order miscounted? Why was the paperwork handled improperly? Ask the responsible employees penetrating questions. Get a small group to analyze and make suggestions for changing the system so these errors do not occur again. Are there problems with paper flow, or are employees inadequately trained? Are there problems with the "process" which keeps employees from doing the job right the first time? Changing your system and training your people to prevent errors, rather than trying to identify and correct them, will improve your customer service and drive down your costs.

The main reason for returned goods was "Customer Refused-Dissatisfied." At 44 percent, this category represents almost half of the reasons for returns. Try interviewing these customers and inside and outside salespeople. Talking with counter salespeople also may help identify why or if customers order the wrong merchandise. Keep in mind that refused shipments cost the customer $40 to $60 also. They should be very interested in knowing how to change their system and thus reduce their costs as well as yours.

The Distributor Must Eliminate Errors

Analyzing the reasons for credit memos being issued can help identify the causes for errors but they must be eliminated not just identified. The only successful method of achieving substantial error reduction over long periods of time is through implementing the quality process. Dr. Deming indicates that the distributor's employees are the only means of changing the system so the errors will not return. They are the only means of finding problems in the system because they are the "experts." It makes sense. Ask yourself, "Who knows more about the warehouse than anyone else?" The answer is the warehouse personnel. The same question should be asked in sales, purchasing, accounting, management, operations, planning, credit, and all other areas of the company. The problem is that many managers have never asked before, but that should not keep you from asking now.

The importance of error reduction and prevention is

vitally important, yet many management teams fail to convince themselves and their employees that job security in a service-oriented business like an industrial wholesaler depends solely on satisfied customers. Distributors must continue to satisfy their customers' needs in order to stay in business. Employees must satisfy customers to keep their jobs. A credit memo or a returned product is a red flag. When too many credit memos are issued or goods are returned, customers are unhappy and will migrate to other distributors who provide better service.

The instrument provided in this chapter should help you learn more about your costs. Take a few minutes to find your costs, and then work to reduce them.

A true reduction can come only from eliminating the number of errors made, called "zero errors productivity". This can best be accomplished by the distributor implementing the "Total Quality Process for Distributors" as developed and taught by the author and his colleagues at Distributor Quality Systems. The process involves changing the distributor systems which cause (allow) 85 percent of the errors which are made. This topic is beyond the scope of this text. However, profit and productivity are not separate issues and will be presented here in the general context of business.

True Cost of Errors is Unknown

Dr. W. Edwards Deming, the internationally famous quality leader, says, "The true cost of errors is unknown and unknowable." He makes this statement because he believes that an unhappy customer tells ten people about his experience, while a completely satisfied customer tells no more than one. The distributor must ask whether or not it lost a customer last year or made one angry. If so, it must be concerned about who the customer is talking to today about the distributor's goods and services. It is reasonable to assume, under these circumstances, that the true cost of errors is unknown and unknowable.

The salvation of any company is its people. Dr. Deming calls them the experts and they are. The distributor must capture their knowledge and expertise.

Returned Goods Cost Matrix

Personnel	Stock	Non-Stock	Your Cost
Inside salesperson	$ 2.50	$ 2.50	
Inside sales supervisor	1.12	1.12	
Error correction clerk	.91	.91	
Shipping clerk	1.12	1.12	
Truck driver	4.50	4.50	
Receiving clerk	.84	.84	
Restocker/order filler	.38	.38	
Vehicle expense			
Average truck expense/return	6.28	6.28	
Average freight to vendor	—	12.10	
Purchasing-buyer	—	3.82	
Data process-keypunch op.	1.50	1.50	
Billing clerk	1.17	1.17	
Accounting clerk	1.35	1.35	
Warehouse manager	—	—	
Receiving supervisor	.84	.84	
Purchasing manager	.50	.50	
Sales manager	1.00	1.00	
Credit manager	.85	.85	
Billing dept. manager	1.05	1.05	
Avg. cost/phone transaction	1.56	1.56	
GROSS EXPENSE	$27.47	$43.39	
(Restocking Charge)	—	—	
NET EXPENSE	$27.47	$43.39	

Twelve

Profit And Productivity

Thomas Jefferson made a wise statement about distributor's personnel even before there were many distributors.

> I know of no safe depository of the ultimate powers of society but the people themselves; and if we think them not enlightened enough to exercise their control with a wholesome discretion the remedy is not to take from them but to inform their discretion by education.

Distributor employees can and do make intelligent decisions when given sufficient information on timely topics.

The purpose of this chapter is to remind the reader that what made this country great, the "free enterprise system," is alive and well. This material will give you some ideas which will help you understand and appreciate the free enterprise system and grow in usefulness by studying how it works. The author believes that you will do a better job for yourself, for your customer, for your company, and for our country if you really understand the economic factors that made this country great in the beginning.

A Historical Perspective

Free enterprise is not something America inherited from other societies. It is something uniquely ours and was a product of the American Revolution. However, some of its basic concepts originated far back in history.

It all began with a man called "Jesus of Nazareth." As a result of his influence, a group was established that became known as Christians. They were persecuted, but the movement could not be destroyed. Finally, one of the Roman emperors, though not a Christian himself, decided if you can not beat them join them. He decreed that everyone in his kingdom would become a Christian regardless of what they believed.

This resulted in the Universal Church which was controlled by the Roman government. Over a period of several hundred years, two factions developed, and the Universal Church split into the Roman Catholic Church and the Greek Orthodox Church. These two churches controlled the political and religious lives of the people for several centuries.

Just like today, the people of that time had many acquaintances, friends and family living in poverty. The people's poverty required that food and other resources be shared and the social doctrine of the church was created. The doctrine was based on the idea that the group was more important than the <u>individual</u>. Consequently, a person was rewarded for the labor based on the size of family, not on how much was produced. Today we call such "sharing the wealth" Socialism and, as an economic system, it has nothing to do with church activities.

As time went on dissension arose, the church split, and a splinter group established what is now known as Protestantism. From this movement came one of the foundations of free enterprise. The "Protestant Work Ethic" says that it is the <u>individual</u> in a society who is of primary importance and not the social <u>group</u>. It also established the idea that a person should be rewarded for what he or she does instead of family size. In America, we have inherited some of both the Catholic Social Doctrine and the Protestant Work Ethic, but we should never lose sight of this time-honored rule, that it is the individual who is important. Distributors should hire the best employees they can find, train them in every aspect of the job, expect a great deal from them, listen and learn from them, then reward them for their accomplishments. The distribution of industrial products is a highly people-intensive industry and it must never be forgotten that people are the distributor's greatest asset.

In 1776, the American Revolution, which was a revolt against the tyranny of the king, established a new government which was dedicated to the importance of individual dignity and human liberties. The Declaration of Independence states, "We hold these truths to be self-evident—that all men are created equal; that they are endowed by the Creator with certain inalienable rights; that among these are life, liberty and the pursuit of happiness."

The revolution also resulted in a new economic system. This system was based upon equality of opportunity, freedom of choice, and the importance of the individual. Because of this, every person in America has the right to improve his or her life by developing his or her own personal abilities and ambitions. Distributors should encourage employees to further develop themselves by obtaining additional education, and distributors should make available to employees a reading list of both technical and personal improvement materials to improve their skills. These books should be available within the company for the employees' use. The distributor should spend from three to seven percent of operating expense on training of employees and further encourage them to get additional education on their own outside the company.

Our original constitution was written to limit the powers of the central government so that the individual could prosper. Although much of this freedom has been undermined by excessive taxation and government regulations, America certainly has prospered and so have our people. Among the world nations, we enjoy one of the highest per person income levels.

However, distributors cannot assume that their employees know, think or talk about these things. Today, many factors threaten the very fundamentals of the free enterprise system which made America great. As Thomas Jefferson said, "The secret to the preservation of our way of life is people who understand and appreciate the Free Enterprise System." The following information is presented to help you understand the basics of free enterprise.

What Is Free Enterprise?

> Free enterprise provides that private business will have the freedom to organize and operate for a profit in a competitive system without interference by government beyond regulation necessary to protect public interest and keep the national economy in balance.

This definition mentions both profit and competition, two important concepts which need to be kept in mind by distributor employees. Employees should understand that profit is essential and that employees, management and the manufacturing partners must work together to produce a healthy profit. Every person in the distributor organization must shoulder part of the responsibility of that profit. As part of the distributor's team you also need to understand that only profit creates job security and that all profits stem from "satisfied customers" and efficient, error-free distributor operations.

In our modern exchange economy, all payrolls and employment come from the customers, and the only worthwhile job security is customer security; if there are no customers, there can be no payroll and no jobs. Customer security can be achieved by the workers only when they cooperate with management in doing the things that win and hold customers. Job security, therefore, is a partnership problem that can be solved only in a spirit of understanding and cooperation. (The Ten Pillars of Economic Wisdom, American Economic Foundation, New York, New York)

Because wholesale distributors operate in a competitive system, errors or other things in your operation which "hassle" your customers must be eliminated. A competitor can and will find a way to do the same job better, with fewer errors and less expense. That competitor must be you! You should set trends, not follow them. You should not sell on price but on value added through providing a quality service. You should *be* the competition.

Of all the economic endeavors in this country, the industrial distributorship owes its lifeblood to free enterprise. What then is free enterprise? First of all, free enterprise is based on the concept that the economic system of a country should serve the people not the government. For example, in a communist or socialistic country the people serve the government. The government writes a "five-year plan" and individuals are expected to conform to this plan. The planners decide which goods and services will be produced and who will produce and distribute them. Because it is a central planning authority, rather than the individuals who make up the society make the economic decisions, they almost never reach their goals. In their system individuals have no incentive to excel.

On the other hand, free enterprise says that the individual is what is important and that it is the individuals who decide how, when and where to invest their skills and money. The free enterprise economy has shown that the individual will make better decisions than some planning committee making decisions for them. This is true because in the free enterprise system profit or loss is the responsibility of each person.

Free Enterprise and Productivity

For almost a century, this country had the highest productivity in the world. The major reason for this lofty position was the free enterprise system. America has lost its competitive edge in productivity in many areas of the economy and the reason is that management and employees no longer practice some of the principles of free enterprise which made America great. The author believes that if distributor personnel understand what has gone wrong and why, they will help get the company and America back on track.

There are four things that a country must have to be productive. They are:

Land: The source of natural resources.

The United States, with only one/seventh of the total land area of the world, has been truly blessed with natural resources. For example, America has 40 percent of the world's coal supply, vast amounts of timber, rich resources of natural gas plus many types of minerals. This is not to say that America is entirely self-sufficient because it does import vast amounts of oil and many minerals from other countries. However, America is generally blessed with a great abundance of natural resources.

Labor: The human effort which transforms natural resources into some useful objects or services.

America is also blessed with a good source of human labor. The pressure which is now being applied to the free enterprise economy is the continual need to reeducate the labor force. For example, in the early 1800s, 90-plus percent of the people in America earned their living on the farm. During the late 1800s and early 1900s, most of them took jobs in factories and became production workers. Today, factories are being automated and workers are being replaced with automatic equipment. Much of this labor force will need to be retrained to operate and repair computer controlled, automated systems and provide other useful services.

Tools: The implements which make man's efforts productive.

The number of tools, their quality and sophistication is limited only by the financial resources and the ingenuity of their developers. Almost every industry which has an opportunity to make a reasonable profit by developing tools will take this risk in order to have the opportunity to generate a profit. Early tools such as the screw, the lever and the wheel are still with us. However, now they are controlled by sophisticated computers and programmable controllers and other items which increase productivity. As tools become more sophisticated, they will require that their operators have more education on a higher level.

Education: The knowledge which allows people to better use tools and resources.

Education is the key ingredient which makes the other three resources work. There are countries in the world which have abundant land, plenty of labor and sufficient tools, but which suffer as very poor countries when compared to America. Although American education has declined in quality during productivity at reasonable levels. However, the new tools will demand that distributors move toward higher education of their people, the greatest use of our natural resources, the most productivity of labor, and the greatest utilization of tools.

It is widely known that the United States has all of these essential ingredients of productivity. Why is it then that we have declined in productivity greatness? Several things come to mind which have caused the country to stray from the straight and narrow path of free enterprise.

- 1 -

America has lost its sense of unity and common purpose as a nation. Our country has become fragmented into pressure groups, each wanting more than its share of the rewards of productivity. Think of it this way. The American gross national product is a pie, which is the total of all goods and services provided to industry and to the people in a given time frame of one year.

Slices of that pie go to each of the various pressure groups in the country. Each of them (including you and me) insists on having as large a piece of the pie as possible. As long as productivity is increasing each group gets more pie each year simply because the pie is getting larger. However, when productivity becomes stagnant, the pie stays the same size or gets smaller, as in a recession. This means that if one group still demands more pie, the only way it will get it is to cut into someone elses share. For example, if distributor employees demand increased wages while productivity growth is zero, they are demanding part of the owners or shareholders part of the pie. They simply cannot receive more unless they give more (contribute to overall economic growth). If they make these demands they have lost sight of a principle of free enterprise which says that "the greatest good for the greatest number means the greatest goods for the greatest number." This, of course, translates to the greatest number of products available at the lowest cost to more people because people making and selling products keep everyone employed. The more we buy, the more we produce, the larger the pie, and the more there is for everyone.

- 2 -

Compliance with the directives of government agencies such as Occupational Safety and Health Act (OSHA), the Environmental Protection Agency (EPA), and the like are taking an even larger share of the economic pie by the increasing demands they place on business. Some of these demands are good, others are not. Regardless of their worth, they cost money to implement and it costs many tax dollars to fund these agencies. Distributor employees and the owners piece of the pie must be decreased to provide for what many believe to be too large a slice of the economic pie government demands to support this bureaucracy.

- 3 -

Inflation is probably the greatest stumbling block to increased productivity, and America has a varied track record of controlling it. Its insidious effects will be with us for a long time. The major cause is elected government officials who refuse to live within a balanced Federal budget. When elected officials refuse to cut governmental programs at a time when America is in a period of declining productivity, these programs are funded with inflated money and everyone suffers because we are taxed more while our dollar is becoming less valuable. This is further compounded by the income tax problem. In the mid 1900s, the average earning power of a distributor salesperson probably put the person in the 20 percent tax bracket. Today, because of inflation, that person may be in a much higher bracket. The individual has no more buying power because the money is worth less.

- 4 -

The fourth item which has a bearing on productivity is tools. Of the four factors of productivity, tools is the only one that can be increased without limit. However, industry will only invest in tools of production when there is an opportunity for profit or a reward for channeling resources into tools. This again creates a vicious circle. Productivity cannot increase unless we have more and better tools of production and in a time of declining productivity we are reluctant to invest in tools, particularly in the unfavorable tax climate in the United States.

This vicious circle needs to be stopped. It can be stopped only by applying the fourth element of productivity, which is education. Distributor personnel must be knowledgeable about the detrimental influence of declining productivity, then be given the challenge to do something about it. Distributor personnel have known for years where the waste was in their operation but no one ever asked them to identify and eliminate it. They will as soon as the distributor educates them in the total quality process and enlists their help. The elimination of errors will improve the satisfaction of customers; they will continue to buy, the distributor will stay in business and provide jobs for employees.

So far we have highlighted the importance of employees understanding free enterprise, traced its history, defined what free enterprise is and looked at the relationship between productivity and free enterprise. We will now examine the five cornerstones of the free enterprise system which distributor employees need to understand.

The Fundamentals of Free Enterprise

Private Property: Private property has a much broader meaning than just private ownership of real estate. Everything the distributor has -- cash, inventories, trucks, receivables, buildings, and its ability to produce services, is the property of that company. Free enterprise says that all property is owned by citizens. The distributorship and all of its assets and liabilities belong to the owners. This property is "private" property not "public" property.

> Government is never a source of goods. Everything produced is produced by the people, and everything that government gives to the people, it must first take from the people. (Ten Pillars of Economic Wisdom, American Economic Foundation, New York, New York.)

It is time for all American citizens to understand that there is "no free lunch." What the government has to give, it must first take from the people. Not one distributor employee can live for an extended period of time without a balanced household budget. Why do we sit idly by and think our government can do so? What are you doing to elect those whom you know will vote accordingly? In addition:

> When property is owned privately, we have an incentive to add to our wealth by becoming property owners and to preserve our wealth by maintaining the quality of our property. The rights of private ownership of property encourage us to work hard and be productive so that we can own property. This productivity leads to economic growth which provides better opportunities for all. (Center of Education and Research in Free Enterprise, Texas A&M University.)

Also, the private ownership of property (inventory, receivables, real estate) means that the distributor has the right to determine how that property is used, to transfer its ownership to someone else, and to enjoy the financial and other rewards it generates or suffer the losses should they occur. This is a far more efficient way of doing business than a system in which the state or society owns the property (communism). It is a simple fact that what we as individuals own we generally maintain. Take public housing projects as an example. If we do not own our property, we have little reason to respect it or care for it. Most people will not deface the walls of their own homes or throw litter on the lawn. Such activity would reduce the value of their private property. Yet, this is unfortunately done regularly to public property. In a very real sense, the employees of a distributorship share in the ownership of that property. If they do quality work and generate satisfied customers, the company will do well and they in turn will have job security.

Economic Freedom: In the free enterprise environment we have the freedom to cooperate with each other in business ventures while at the same time serving our own private interests. The manufacturer-distributor relationship is a good example. Distributors are free to try to represent the most successful manufacturers, who are also free to sell through the best distributors they can attract. This is "economic freedom" and is as basic to the American heritage as freedom of speech, freedom of religion, the right to own and bear arms and the other guaranteed freedoms. Economic freedom means that distributors have the right to open a new branch, close a branch, invest in any inventory or equipment they can afford and use new technology to produce and market the products they choose.

Distributor employees should also understand that the free enterprise system does not guarantee success because customers have rights also. We do not have a profit system in America; it is a <u>profit or loss system</u>. Our customers have the right to buy any product they like, change suppliers, buy any goods or services they can afford at as low a price (or cost) as they can find, and use their resources in any manner they desire as long as they don't conflict with the rights of others. Today's intelligent buyers will buy where they get the best products and services which are produced by those distributors who provide these products and services with the fewest errors and hassles. These distributors will be the "low cost suppliers" and will stay in business while the others are being eliminated. How well do you as an employee understand these principles? Do you understand that the only <u>job security is based on customer satisfaction and that the customer's satisfaction is your personal responsibility</u>?

Economic freedom is very important to distributor employees. Although they have no guarantee of success, economic freedom allows them to strive to accomplish what is in their best interest. Working toward self-motivated goals, such as promotion, more responsibility and thus, higher salary, encourages people to be productive. When people are productive, companies and nations are productive, and everyone has a higher standard of living.

Economic Incentive: It is a fact of human nature that we need a stimulus to get us to accomplish something. There are very few things in life that get done without a "WIIFM" or "what's in it for me." Even things we do in the name of religion or helping our fellow man often have as their impetus the reward of the self-satisfaction we feel for having done something good and unselfish.

Certainly one of the things that makes free enterprise work is economic incentive. An employee who works for a distributor can have the incentive of a promotion to a management position and reap the rewards by accepting more responsibility. At the same time distributors have the incentive of acquiring a larger share of the market and making more profit. Your customers will have an incentive to buy from you if your quality is higher and/or your service is better and/or the total cost to do business with you is lower.

Economic freedom for the distributor, coupled with the incentive concept for employees, allows each to proceed along an economic path which will be most beneficial to all.

The distributor's salary incentive program for employees, when implemented properly, should encourage them to be more productive and more efficient. The salesperson who learns how to cover the territory more efficiently, contacts more customers and makes more sales, will consequently make higher commissions than a less efficient one. Of course, the incentive is not always money. It might be recognition, a more prestigious job, a better company car, better working conditions and the like. However, the idea of incentive or rewards also includes punishments which distributor employees must understand. In our system, if a person fails to do the job, the result is a low salary or perhaps dismissal. Companies also can go out of business if they do not produce what their customers require. Employees need to be constantly evaluated to determine how well they are fulfilling customers needs.

> All payroll and employment comes from the customers, and the only worthwhile job security is customer security; if there are no customers, there can be no payroll and no jobs. (The Ten Pillars of Economic Wisdom, American Economic Foundation, New York, New York)

Economic incentives are essential if a free enterprise system is to function. Employees should be stimulated and educated to reduce the waste in their operations, which in turn will increase their productivity and both they and the company will benefit because the low cost producer will keep customers over long periods of time. Employers have the incentive to reward employees when the result of less waste and fewer errors is higher profits and better satisfied customers.

The Competitive Marketplace: Recently, the author attended a distributors' association annual convention. A highlight of the convention was the day set aside for manufacturer and distributor executives to discuss business in an informal booth arrangement. The distributors are assigned to booths, and manufacturers choose whom they will visit. At another meeting the role is reversed and the manufacturers are in the booths and the distributors visit the manufacturers they want to see. This is a practical illustration of the competitive market aspect of free enterprise. The key to the two conventions is that both manufacturers and distributors were free to decide whom to visit and what to discuss. Free enterprise works on the basis that what is produced in a society is the goods and services most valued by the individual consumers of that society. If we provide a service which is necessary, valuable, and economically beneficial we will have customers. If we do not, we will not have customers or business and there will be no jobs.

For the competitive market to work, there must be a communications system so that the distributors of goods and services can react to the desires and needs of the consumers in that society. The communications process takes place when buyers and sellers meet in a competitive market. A competitive market requires that there be sufficient buyers and sellers so that no one buyer or seller is large enough to control the market. Distributors to our knowledge have always seemed to fit this pattern, for competition abounds.

In a pure free enterprise system, we as individuals answer the questions of what to produce, how to produce, and how to divide. (Center for Education and Research in Free Enterprise, Texas A&M University.)

This is good because our competitive markets allow us to use our economic freedoms. Both the buyer and the seller have the freedom to decide who to sell through or from whom to buy. Each must receive a benefit from the transaction or they will buy from or sell through someone else.

Limited Role of Government: Since free enterprise as an economic system is based on the freedoms and rights of individuals, it follows that this system is one of supply and demand. If the system works, then, by necessity the role of the government must be limited.

The government, if free enterprise is to be viable, must have only three functions: 1) it makes the rules (laws); 2) it enforces the rules, and 3) it arbitrates the rules.

The laws which are passed should always protect the individual manufacturers, distributors and consumers who buy or sell in whatever market they choose. This insures the promotion of a competitive marketplace. When the rules are broken, then the government is responsible for taking corrective action. When there are disputes concerning different interpretations of the rules, the government acts as the arbitrator to settle these disputes. These are the only economic roles of government in a free enterprise system. Anything else is a violation of the sacred right of individuals to make the economic decisions. The government should provide a structure so that individual distributorships have equal opportunities to function in the free marketplace. Government must not participate in answering the "what to produce," "how to produce," and "how to divide" questions. Neither must it impose such strenuous regulations that it strangles the free enterprise system. Employees should learn about the regulations which are harmful to distributors. You should write and ask your congressman to vote accordingly.

Conclusion

What has been presented here is not new or unique. However, many times we think we know something, but fail to really understand the true facts. A friend of ours said recently that America has all of the know-how and technology that any other country has. What we have lost is the discipline to apply what we know. Also, perhaps some of us have forgotten or lost sight of what this great country is all about. Free enterprise is what made us, and free enterprise will continue to be the mechanism that keeps this the greatest country in the world. Free enterprise and the quality process are sermons worth preaching constantly. The author hopes that you will take this information seriously and use it to provide better service for your customers!

Thirteen

The Computer As A Distributor Management Tool

Those wholesalers and distributors who do not have a computerized management information system have found it increasingly difficult to continue to control costs and operate their businesses at a profit. Those companies with computers are finding that systems developed specifically for distributors are no longer a luxury but rather are necessary for insuring sustained growth, increased profitability, and in some cases, survival itself.

Functional Areas

There are five functional areas within an industrial distributor's operation where a computer can assist in better managing the business. These functional areas are sales order processing, inventory management, purchase order processing, accounts payable and receivable, and general ledger.

Depth of Solution

Levels of sophistication vary from one computer system to another. Actually it is not so much the computer or hardware itself, but the software programs running on the computer that determine how effectively the overall system helps the distributor's employees do their jobs. While most systems provide the basic five functions listed above, some computer software programs provide much more detail or "depth of solution" than others do. Depth of solution is a measure of the ability of the computer to provide a distributor's employees with help provided by the computer in a given functional area.

While the computer software programs determine how effective a distributor's computer system will be, software must be closely matched to the computer hardware. The names "hardware" and "software" themselves are quite descriptive. Hardware is the physical computer itself consisting of the computer components, terminals, and printers. Software is the program or set of instructions that tells the computer what to do.

Hardware

Computer hardware consists of a processing unit, an information storage unit, and information input/output units. These components function together to provide the information needed by the distributor. The main processor is really the heart of the computer. The processor, often called the central processing unit or CPU, is designed to do a certain type of computing. The design of computers used by industrial distributors is characterized by CPUs that will handle large volumes of repetitive transactions with many employees simultaneously using the computer. As more and more information is simultaneously processed by the computer, the central processing unit tends to slow down. This is an indication that hardware replacement may be needed in the near future.

The main memory of the computer is contained in the central processing unit and serves as a work space in which processing takes place. Both the software program instructions and the distributors data being processed are held in the main memory of the computer. The size of the main memory is measured in megabytes (millions of bytes) or gigabytes (billions of bytes). Generally a byte is the amount of memory needed to hold one piece of information. The size of the computer's memory plays an important role in determining the capacity of the computer as well as the speed at which it processes transactions.

Disk drives connected to the central processing unit accomplish the function of information storage. Once stored it can be retrieved for processing. Modern disk drives consist of multiple platters of magnetic media stacked one above another. Intervening spaces between each platter allow recording heads to read and write to both the top and the bottom of each disk. The speed at which disk drives can retrieve information determines in part how fast the overall computer system operates.

An important part of information storage is the concept of information backup. Information backups, or copies, involve data and programs stored on the computer systems disk drives. These copies are made periodically to insure that valuable business data is not lost due to disk drive failures during operation. Most distributors perform these backups on a daily basis and store these sets in different physical locations. In this manner valuable data is protected against disasters such as fire or flood.

The final components associated with an industrial distributor's computer hardware are the data input and output devices. Data input is most often accomplished via a terminal or cathode ray tube (CRT) equipped with a keyboard. Information is typed on the keyboard to answer questions or fill in blanks displayed on the terminal's screen. Bar code scanners and electronic data interchange (EDI) are being used to automatically enter data by most distributors. These current technologies allow industrial distributors to enter data more quickly and more accurately.

CRT terminals are the most common computer output device. Many types of reports and other computer-generated information can be viewed by a user as needed on the CRT screen. The printer is another type of computer output device. Printers are used to generate a variety of reports on computer paper as well as checks used to pay both vendors and employees.

Systems Software

Computer software programs must be classified as two types. The first type is called systems software or simply "the operating system." These programs are designed to operate a specific computer. The operating system is the set of instructions which link the computer hardware and the software which accomplish the data processing.

Applications Software

The applications software is the key to how well the computer improves the productivity of the distributor's employees. The software programs can help accomplish this increase in productivity by decreasing the amount of paper which must flow from department to department within the distributorship and by making better information available for decision-making purposes.

Most applications software programs can be classified as integrated or nonintegrated. Integrated software uses a single piece of data to change multiple pieces of information within the computer. For instance, consider the entry of a customer order into a distributor's computer which uses integrated applications software. When someone has entered the order, the computer automatically accomplishes a number of tasks. First a picking-shipping ticket is printed on a printer in the warehouse causing the items contained on the customer's order to be picked, packed and shipped to the customer. Next, the computer causes an invoice to be created for the purposes of billing the customer. This invoice may not be printed at this time, but it is created showing that the customer must be billed at some later date. The creation of the invoice triggers an increase in the industrial distributor's accounts receivable for that customer showing that a sale has taken place and that the customer owes the distributor for the amount of the sale. Finally, the computer deducts the items contained on the customer order from inventory quantity on hand to reflect the fact that the distributor removed inventory from the shelf and shipped it to the customer. To finish this integrated transaction, the computer updates the sales history file to show which customer bought what product on what day. The sales history file may then be used to drive an automated purchasing system and to help the distributor predict sales of specific items in the future. Or, the point of sale data could be used in a vendor managed inventory system to inform the suppliers that these items were sold.

Functional Areas

As previously discussed, there are five basic functional areas in any distribution business. The computer's power can be brought to bear in each of these functional areas in order to increase overall employee productivity. Productivity increases and improved customer service are the most important rationales for having a computer system.

Sales Order Processing

The process of taking, recording and filling sales orders normally begins with inside or counter sales in an industrial distributorship. The nature of this process has changed considerably over the past few years. In some geographic areas customers buy more often on the basis of some personal relationship with a specific distributor salesperson. In other areas customers are more apt to buy on the basis of price. Industrial distributors must continually move from competing on the basis of price and seek to compete on fulfilling the specific needs of the customer. One way for the industrial distributor to do this is to provide high levels of service in the sales order-taking process. The distributor's computer, given properly designed applications software, can provide the distributor's inside and outside salespeople with a competitive advantage in providing improved service for their customers.

Three basic subfunctions must take place in the sales order processing function: order entry, bidding or quoting, and look-up of product availability and price. Order entry is the subfunction that accommodates the direct entry of customer orders into the computer system. The quoting or bidding subfunction allows a customer to inquire about pricing and availability for needed products and receive written confirmation of that pricing and availability. The inquiry subfunction is an on-line look-up of the on-shelf quantity of items available for sale and shows both the quantities and price. These three subfunctions should be integrated so that an inquiry of available quantities and prices for a particular item can be converted to an order without reentering the information.

Order entry should be designed to make it easy for the salesperson to enter a customer order. Screens should be laid out in a manner that will facilitate entering all of the information necessary to process and ship the order to the customer in a timely fashion. The ability to serve the customer very quickly then becomes the basis for improved competition, rather than price alone.

The system should be designed so that the inside salesperson is prompted to get all required information from the customer. It should also provide maximum information to the inside salesperson who can answer customer questions about availability of product and pricing.

For instance, if a customer calls in to place an order, and if the order requires a purchase order number for billing, the system should not allow the salesperson to go forward with entry of the order without securing that purchase order number from the customer. In a similar fashion, other pertinent data such as ship-to addresses and basic billing information should be shown on the order entry screen. As the customer reads off the list of items, the system should force the salesperson to ask for needed data regarding individual items. For instance, industrial distributorships are characterized by highly technical products requiring extensive description as to voltage levels and power requirements. When a customer is ordering such an item, the system should require the salesperson to input the specifications necessary to insure that the customer receives the correct materials. An order entry screen which requires these critical specifications to be entered can improve customer satisfaction and save the distributor and the customer much expense and frustration.

Properly designed order processing software can enable the industrial distributor to provide improved service to the customer in a number of other ways. The average industrial distributor maintains some 40,000 inventory items in the warehouse. Many of these items are classified as commodities, which means that they do not vary in form, functionality or specification between manufacturers. In this case, substitutions for one manufacturer's item by that of another manufacturer may be permitted by the customer. In cases where delivery of the item in the least amount of time is critical to the customer, commodities will indeed be substituted across manufacturers' lines. To facilitate these substitute items, the computer should make available at the time of order entry a list of direct substitutions. When a customer orders item XYZ and specifies a manufacturer or a brand name and that item is not available, the inside sales-person can tell the customer immediately that a substitute is available. In those cases where there are no direct substitutes for commodity items, there may be items that can be shipped immediately which represent a higher quality or more powerful or higher capacity that will accomplish the same function as the product ordered by the customer. In these cases where delivery time is critical, the system should prompt the inside salesperson as to the availability of this higher-priced upgrade that could be used by the customer in the absence of the product that was ordered.

Properly designed order entry software allows identification of particular items held in inventory by a variety of item numbers. Customers may want to order specific items by using their own item numbers rather than the manufacturer's or the distributor's item number. In these cases, software systems for order processing must be able to identify each item by several item numbers. This provides a way for an industrial distributor to add value to the product being sold to the customer. No longer does the customer have to determine the distributor's or the manufacturer's item number, but when offered this service, can place the orders based upon the customer's own item numbers.

The second major requirement for a sales order entry system on the computer is to provide for inquiries concerning quantities of the product available for sale and current pricing of that product. Many times when a customer calls to place an order, the shipment will be required immediately and in the full quantity ordered. If the distributor is unable to ship a particular product in the required quantity, the customer may want to place the order with a different distributor. Given these requirements for shipping complete and considering the fact that it is not uncommon for industrial distributors to stock 40,000 inventory items, the computer must allow the salesperson to quote quantities available and prices almost instantaneously. Sales order systems on a computer can accomplish this task by allowing the inside salesperson to enter a part number or generic description of an item wanted by a customer and having the computer display balance on hand in inventory, protected stock, and quantity available for sale. If a part is not available in inventory, the customer can be informed immediately as to when it will be available. This implies a system that can access the purchase order processing subsystem to determine the next date of delivery based upon outstanding purchase orders for that particular product.

At the time of inquiry about price and availability of product the computer must allow the inside salesperson to process the customer's order for the product at the press of a button. Simply entering the desired quantity of this item is all that should be required. It should be noted that information regarding availability and pricing has a definite value to the customer. The ability of the distributor to provide this information almost instantaneously is a service for which some customers are willing to pay.

In times when customers are buying on price alone, industrial distributors receive requests for quotations for large orders from their customers. To facilitate timely and accurate bids, the computer system should allow entry of a formal bid which is much the same as entry of a formal order. The bid information should be accumulated and each line item should be listed along with the quantity and price. This provides a total quote for the package of products that the customer desires. The quote should list a range of dates during which the quoted prices will be guaranteed. It should be stored in the computer for that period of time. When the distributor gets the order that is based upon a previous quote, the sales order entry system should allow the inside salesperson to retrieve the quote and turn it into a normal order. No rekeying of either specific product numbers or quantities should be required.

Finally, the well-designed order processing system should allow a salesperson to inquire about the status of an order previously placed by a customer. Oftentimes, the customer who has called to place an order will make an inquiry as to when previous order(s) was shipped. At this point, the inside salesperson should have to do nothing more than enter the customer's purchase order number to see the record displayed on the screen. If the customer does not have a P.O. number, the system should list all open orders for that customer and allow the salesperson to choose an order or orders for review.

The sales order processing system provides an interface between the customer and the industrial distributor. The customer's perception of the capabilities of the distributor are greatly affected by how well the sales order entry process works. If the inside salesperson, supported by the proper sales order processing system on the computer, can provide the customer substitutes for items they are trying to order and the availability of particular items, as well as prices, and can seemingly do this instantaneously for a very large number of products, the customer's perceptions of the distributorship are enhanced. On the other hand, if the customer must endure long waits, or if salespeople are unfamiliar with substitutes, the customer's ideas about how effective the distributor is in satisfying immediate needs will be understandably negatively affected. The computer system can greatly influence the customer's perceptions of the quality service provided by the distributor by making it quick and easy for the customer to place an order.

Inventory Management

The primary way that a distributorship adds value to products sold is having them available in sufficient quantities at the appropriate location when the customer wants to buy them. To do this, the distributor must maintain an inventory of the items desired by the customer. Dollar value of this inventory typically will exceed all other assets within a distributorship. It will be approached in value only by accounts receivable. Since so many of the distributor's resources are tied up in inventory, the computer system should be designed specifically with the idea of managing that resource. Successful implementation of inventory management demands high levels of service at the lowest possible cost. Perfect inventory management would be a system that always had every product that the customer wanted to buy in stock and could do that at zero cost. This is clearly unobtainable. There are, however, computer systems that enable the distributor to maximize service to the customer by having the needed inventory at the proper time and do it at the minimum cost.

Inventory management systems revolve around the ability of the computer to collect data on past sales of the product.

This historical record of past sales is used to predict the most likely level of future sales. These predictions of future sales are used by the computer to approximate the appropriate stocking levels for each particular item.

For any specific product that a distributor chooses to stock, there are two decisions that must be made. The first is when to place a replenishment order for that product. The second is how many of that product the distributor should buy. It is important to note that these two decisions are typically made separately. The decision of when to place a replenishment order for a product determines the service level which can be provided to customers. The decision of how many of a specific product to buy is determined by the "cost to buy" vs. the "cost to stock" (and own) that particular item.

Customer service is provided when the order is placed and the customer is informed that the product can be shipped immediately. The service level can be measured quite easily and the computer will accumulate this data automatically. Traditionally, the level of service provided to customers is computed by counting the total number of lines on sales orders that were shipped complete in some given period, and dividing that figure by the total lines from sales orders during the same period.

Appropriate levels of service should be in the 90 percent to 97 percent range. Levels of service much below these contribute to decreased distributor profits through lost sales. Levels of service much above 97 percent contribute to decreased distributor profits due to excessively high inventory carrying costs. The properly designed inventory management system on the computer will accumulate and report the service levels on an item-by-item basis as well as a product line basis.

The quantities of a particular product that a distributor holds in inventory will greatly affect the cost of carrying that inventory. Large quantities equate to large costs. The computer accumulates data regarding the past demand or sales for those products. The properly designed inventory management system will automatically calculate suggested stocking levels on a product by product basis.

The industrial distributor's computer system also assists in controlling costs through identification of dead stock. Dead stock is defined as those inventory items which are not selling. Reports generated by the computer which contain a listing of those items that do not sell enable the distributor to remove this so called "dead stock," thus freeing up space in the warehouse, reducing the total dollar amount of inventory upon which the distributor has to pay taxes, and reducing the investment in inventory.

Purchase Order Processing

The third functional area within an industrial distributorship where the computer plays a part in improving productivity is in purchase order processing. The purchasing department issues purchase orders to suppliers to replenish inventory in response to diminished inventory levels in the warehouse. The sales order processing subsystem, the inventory management subsystem, and the purchase order processing subsystem are very closely linked in the computer. Sales orders and their processing reduce levels of inventory in the warehouse. In exactly the opposite manner, the processing of purchase orders and the receipt of materials increase inventory in the warehouse. The process of replenishment of inventory seems simple. As levels of a particular item decrease over time through sales, the purchasing department places an order for that item with a supplier, thus increasing levels of that product both in the warehouse and in the computer. The realities of purchasing, however, dictate dealing with tens of thousands of products which are bought and sold in different quantities and from different suppliers. Often, combinations of items must be purchased from a particular supplier to achieve some economic advantage such as reduced price or free freight. The industrial distributor buys from so many suppliers that it becomes impossible to evaluate each supplier's individual inventory items each day with regard to issuing a purchase order for replenishment from that supplier.

The purchase order processing subsystem helps the distributor order more efficiently. This subsystem is used to determine available-for-sale quantities contained in inventory.

As these quantities reach a point called the order point, the purchase order processing subsystem is triggered to begin accumulating all those items that are at or below the order point for a particular supplier. The computer then issues a report to the purchasing department containing these items. The report is generally called a "recommended buy report" and alerts the purchasing department to the fact that if they do not place orders for these items immediately, those items remaining will be sold prior to replenishment stock arriving. The buyers at the industrial distributorship can review the items contained on this recommended buy report, change quantities on items as needed, and delete items or add items as appropriate. If the recommended buy report meets the buyer's approval, it can be turned into a purchase order with a few keystrokes. At this time the computer will print the hard copy of the purchase order to be mailed, or send the order directly to the manufacturer's computer by one or more telecommunications methods.

The computer also can be programmed so that each supplier's items in inventory are reviewed for replenishment purposes at specified intervals. This technique, called line buying, allows the distributor to order any number of items from a manufacturer's complete line. This system has many economic advantages for the distributor.

The purchase order processing subsystem in the computer tracks other information which is very important to the industrial distributor and the customers, such as lead time, on an item-by-item basis. Lead time, usually measured in days, is that period of time between the moment an industrial distributor orders the items and the point in time when those items arrive and are placed on the shelf ready for sale. Lead times are important because they help establish when to place an order for a particular item for replenishment. Items that have short supplier lead times are treated much differently in the purchasing process than those items that have very long lead times. Obviously, an item with a very long lead time must be ordered far in advance of an item with a very short lead time. To calculate the proper lead times, the computer keeps track of the date on which the purchase order was issued and the date on which first receipt of material on that purchase order was noted. The difference between these two dates becomes the last lead time for that particular purchase order and the products on that purchase order.

Lead time experienced by the distributor for replenishment of a particular item or group of items is also used to provide customers with information regarding when they can expect delivery of items they are ordering. The expected arrival date of each purchase order issued is the lead time calculated by the computer. When a customer calls to inquire about an item that is not in stock but is on order, the salesperson can give the customer an idea of when the item will be available. Many computer systems make the estimated date of arrival of all outstanding purchase orders for an item available on the inventory inquiry screen.

Accounts Receivable and Payable

Accounts receivable represents money owed to the industrial distributor by customers to whom merchandise was sold but for which they have not paid. Accounts payable represents money the distributor owes to suppliers arising from the purchase of inventory for which it has not yet paid. Accounts receivable increase as a result of selling, processing and shipping orders. Accounts payable will rise as a process of issuing purchase orders and receiving merchandise from suppliers. Accounts receivable are decreased when the distributor's customers send checks or transfer funds in payment for the merchandise which has been shipped to them previously. Accounts payable are decreased when the distributor issues checks to the suppliers in payment for inventory which it has received from them. Because industrial distributors typically have thousands of customers and hundreds of suppliers, a distributor's computer system can greatly increase the efficiency with which these accounts are processed.

Accounts Receivable

When a customer places an order with the industrial distributor, the sales order processing subsystem must make an inquiry of the accounts receivable subsystem to see whether or not the customer has paid past bills on time. This inquiry can take several forms. One form states whether the customer has owed the distributor money for longer than 30 or 60 days. Another form indicates whether or not the customer's current purchases plus unpaid past bills are greater than the customer's established credit limit. By using these inquiries into accounts receivable at the time the customer is placing an order, the distributor can identify those customers who represent a higher than desired credit risk and sell to them on a cash basis only.

The accounts receivable subsystem also supplies the industrial distributor with reports listing customers and their payment histories. These lists of payment history are useful in evaluating and identifying customers who are falling behind in paying their bills. These customers can be targeted for more stringent collection procedures. Because the computer is able to identify slow paying customers out of a large customer base, the distributor can concentrate the collection efforts where they will do the most good.

The accounts receivable subsystem can estimate, based on past payment histories, the amount of cash receipts that should be expected from customers for each working day in the future. These estimates of cash inflows are extremely useful to managers in the industrial distributorship for establishment of the timing of payment of suppliers, as well as for estimating the need to borrow to cover short-term shortages of cash in the future.

The computerized accounts receivable subsystem is

also responsible for the printing of monthly statements to be mailed to the industrial distributor's customers. These statements of purchases during the past month serve as bills to the customers. The statements list each invoice created by the computer during the sales order entry process by date, invoice number and total amount. The total amount printed at the bottom of the statement represents the total amount of merchandise bought by the customer during the past month for which payment is expected. These statements are printed automatically each month for all the industrial distributor's customers who request them, thus greatly enhancing the efficiency of the billing process.

Accounts Payable

The computerized accounts payable subsystem accumulates the amount of money owed by the distributor to suppliers for inventory ordered from those suppliers. First, when we cut (print) a purchase order it is noted by the accounts payable subsystem. When the supplier sends an invoice requesting payment for the items shipped it is entered into the accounts payable subsystem and automatically matched to the purchase order. At this point, the shipment may not have arrived at the distributor's receiving dock. If this is the case, the computerized accounts payable subsystem typically will not approve the bill for payment. As the merchandise arrives at the receiving dock, the distributor checks the merchandise. The computer matches this check list and the original purchase order against the invoice from the supplier. Shortages and overages in item quantities are noted by the computer as well as differences in prices contained on the purchase order and the suppliers invoice. If discrepancies exist, the accounts payable subsystem will alert the purchasing department of the problem. Otherwise, the invoice sent to the distributor by the supplier is placed in line for payment.

These invoices typically are not paid immediately. The supplier generally has established terms for payment. These terms describe the amount of time a distributor can delay payment of an invoice as well as the terms for taking a cash discount. The cash discount is an amount the distributor may deduct from the stated invoice in return for prompt payment. For instance, the supplier's payment terms may allow the distributor to delay payment for 30 days but offer a two percent discount off the total invoice amount for payment within 10 days. This payment term is known in the distribution industry as 2/10/net 30.

The properly designed and utilized accounts payment subsystem can greatly improve the management of cash in an industrial distributorship by providing managers with information regarding how much cash will be needed for the on-time payment of suppliers on each future business day.

General Ledger

General ledger is the last major subsystem in an industrial distributors software package. General ledger can be thought of as the subsystem that maintains the overall accounting records for the business. General ledger takes the totals from all other subsystems and integrates them into the financial statements common to all businesses. These statements are called the income statement, the balance sheet, and the statement of changes in financial position.

The income statement is a compilation of all of the revenue-producing activities as well as expenses incurred by the distributorship during a given period of time. The numerical difference between the revenues generated through sales and total expenses incurred during a period of time is called net income before tax. Income taxes which must be paid are subtracted from this amount which then shows the net income after tax. Net income after tax is the most basic measure of how well the industrial distributor is managing the business. The income statement with all of its detail is used by managers to evaluate levels of sales by category and product line as well as levels of expenses incurred to accomplish these sales. Changes in sales levels as well as changes in expenses relative to sales levels can be detected by managers of an industrial distributor by comparing income statements covering two consecutive periods of time. These changes are often good, as in the case where sales are increasing faster than expenses are increasing.

The real value of the income statement, however, is to alert managers to changes in levels of sales or expenses which over time may represent potential difficulties to the business. The computerized general ledger subsystem allows managers of the industrial distributorship to automatically print for review the results of operations of the business on a daily, weekly or monthly basis through the compilation of income statements covering these periods of time. Without the computer, the generation of these documents would be an extremely time-consuming chore.

The balance sheet is a document that is used along with the income statement to indicate how efficiently an industrial distribution business is operating. This balance sheet can be thought of as a snapshot in time of the assets and liabilities as well as the levels of the owner's investment in the distributorship. On the balance sheet, the total dollar amount of the assets minus the total dollar amount of the liabilities will always equal the amount of the owner's investment in the business. This balance between assets, liabilities and owner's investment gives rise to the name "balance sheet".

Assets on the balance sheet are all items of value owned by the distributor, including cash in the bank, inventory, buildings and land, office and warehouse equipment, as well as the computer system itself. Liabilities include all amounts owed to others, including accounts payable to suppliers and monies borrowed from banks.

The balance sheet provides information to managers regarding the amount of assets required to generate the income reported on the income statement. Information from both the income statement and the balance sheet can be combined to calculate the return on investment realized by the owners of the company. As with the income statement, the computerized general ledger subsystem will automatically print, for management review, balance sheets based on any point in time to correspond with income statements covering that period of time. This allows managers to better evaluate the operations of the business.

The statement of changes in financial position is the last type of financial statement provided by the computerized general ledger subsystem. This statement provides managers with information regarding how assets were utilized during specific periods of time. Further discussion of the statement of changes in financial position is generally beyond the scope of this text.

By automatically reporting the results of distributor operations over time, the computerized general ledger subsystem relieves distributor employees of the task of accumulating these numbers by hand. Before the advent of the computerized general ledger process, generation of financial statements and posting transactions to the proper accounts was much more tedious and time consuming than it is today.

Conclusions

The computer system is one of the most powerful productivity tools the industrial distributor possesses. The computer system affects all areas of operation within a business. These areas range from sales order entry to inventory management and to purchasing, as well as accounts receivable and payable. The computer system relieves the distributor's employees from dull and error-prone tasks such as entering sales orders and other accounting transactions to the proper accounts by hand. The industrial distributor's computer system provides the enormous computing power to automatically handle huge inventories in the most efficient manner. While the employees and their abilities will always be the distributor's number one asset, the distributor's computer system clearly is the next most valuable asset.

The distributor's computer system and the ability of the employees to utilize the system to more efficiently manage the business in the future will be the key to maintaining profitability in the industrial distributorship. The consideration of the purchase or change of a company computer system, like other business decisions, must deliver a clear payback to the industrial distributor in order to justify the investment in time, dollars and continuing expense. Since information management does not in itself represent a profit opportunity, how can the investment be justified? The answer is enhanced productivity and improved customer service.

Enhancing the productivity of people, inventory and sales activities can significantly increase the return on investment of an industrial distributorship. By continuing to optimize the elements of productivity of your key assets and resources, the company will respond to market opportunities, better satisfy customer needs, and give the owners their greatest return on invested capital. The properly designed computer system will allow industrial distributors to do all of these things now and in the future.

Fourteen

The Early Years

All distributor and manufacturer personnel should make themselves aware of the history of the distribution industry because history reveals that modern day distribution is an outgrowth of people trying desperately to meet an industrial need. The forerunners of our present day distributors were people known as peddlers. They played an important part in the structure of industrial America.

Much of the industrial America we know today was started on the eastern seaboard. As America grew and moved westward, there came an ever increasing-need for goods and services. The goods which were made in the East needed to be transported to where they were needed farther west. A primary source of movement of these goods in the early days was the peddler. He stocked his wagon and risked his money, and often his life, to bring the merchandise he had purchased for resale to the people in the western states. The peddler was a rugged individualist, braving the elements and the bad weather, as well as possible Indians, thieves and robbers. The "peddler" was a private business-man, an entrepreneur. He bought the goods, paid for them with hard-earned money, and transported them. The peddler owned his own merchandise, took a financial risk, and earned his profits as a reward for the chances he took. Although the peddler's goods could hardly be considered contractor or industrial supplies, today's wholesale distributor performs the same functions and assumes similar risks.

As the country grew in population, small towns were developed and with them came the more recognizable general store, taking away the need for the peddler and his goods. However, the peddlers were men of flexibility and ingenuity and quickly changed their method of operation. They began to join themselves with manufacturers who became more aware of their particular services. The manufacturers, recognizing the talents of the peddler, began to extend him credit and provide him with consigned merchandise. With consigned merchandise, the peddler did not have to pay for the material until he sold it. Since the peddler did not have to invest as much of his own money, he could now afford a larger inventory and his business flourished. As the manufacturers began to assist the peddler with his inventory, he began to pick out lines which he particularly liked and was good at selling, and specialized in those lines. He developed valuable information and built a strong reputation for knowing his product and its application.

One example of successful peddling was that of Diamond Jim Brady, the 19th century's greatest supply salesperson. His approach to selling railroad equipment supplies was simple: "Nothing succeeds like success." He earned his name and reputation because he spent half of what he earned from selling on looking professional and on expensive diamonds. He was yesterday's most knowledgeable salesperson and had tremendous business acumen and common sense. The one-time New York bellboy left behind a tradition of salesmanship still felt today.

With his new skills the peddler also got a new name. He had become a "drummer." He was called a drummer because he had specialized knowledge and "beat the same drum" wherever he went.

In the early 1820s, a number of events took place, starting with the invention of the boring bar which allowed the development of Watt's steam engine. Piston holes could now be bored instead of hand filed, a process which improved the efficiency of the engine and led to the development of the steam locomotive. The advent of rail transportation spurred the improvement of the steel industry which became a reality through the Bessemer converter. These inventions were all a part of the development of the transportation industry. The railroad as a means of rapid transportation discontinued the need for the drummer and his wagon in many portions of the country. However, with the railroad came the need for railroad supplies. As the railroads grew, they not only delivered supplies but also consumed large amounts of supplies themselves. The opportunity arose to sell not only railroad supplies but also mill supplies where raw materials were being processed.

Even though the modern distribution industry had its early roots in the Industrial Revolution of the 1820s, its growth was slow and had no particular strength until around 1850. Even then, distributors were scarce until the Civil War.

With the onset of the Civil War, industry made tremendous demands for uniforms, ammunition, guns and other items of war. The demands the Civil War put on society brought forth floods of inventions. New devices such as the disc cultivator, the cream separator, and the horse-drawn combine provided jobs for thousands of workers in the industrial centers. The Bessemer Converter was soon to be replaced by the open-hearth furnace, and college-trained metallurgists developed high-speed steel. Tremendous strides were made in the American economy between 1860 and 1900 through the development of patents on these inventions.

During this period in American history, another industry was emerging -- the electrical industry. It began in the 1880s as people came to realize that the electric lamp was safe, practical and here to stay.

Carbon lamps began to replace gas lamps, and the selling of these lamps to homes, stores, offices and factories became a big business. As most big businesses prospered, problems began to occur and the electrical industry had its share.

The wholesale distributor, or "jobber," experienced chaos as more and more varieties of products were developed. Its associates — the contractors and the engineers — were also confused about the coming electrical era.

The "jobber's association" was formed in the Midwest in order to combat some of the rising pricing problems. Soon this group linked with the Eastern and Western groups and began to write national policies and standards. This pioneering effort later became the National Association of Electrical Distributors (NAED).

The early products of the industrial distributor were such things as lubricating oil, wiping rags, leather belts, belt lacings, fasteners, files, hand tools and grinding wheels. The mill supply house became a reality in the years between 1860 and 1900. It was called the mill supply house because it provided supplies to all types of milling operations from flour mills to textile mills.

As the general store was the forerunner of the mill supply house, the peddler and the drummer were forerunners of the industrial salesperson. As the demand increased for specialized tools and supplies and the need arose for a more knowledgeable person to sell and service these supplies, that person was the mill supply salesperson. During the competitive years following the Civil War, salespeople became an essential part of the marketplace because their selling techniques matched the new markets.

Like the peddler and the drummer, the salesperson in the 1870s and 1880s was a hearty individual. He traveled his territory on horseback, in stagecoaches, on flatboats, sometimes in buggies, and, where available, by steam locomotive. Since most of the industrial plants of his customers were located along railroad tracks, he literally walked miles and miles along these tracks. He was an intelligent individual, quick with a pencil and deeply steeped in industrial applications. At night he settled for meager accommodations, often lodging with two or three other salesmen in a single room. Clean sheets were pure luxury.

By the early 1900s, even though he still had tremendous price competition to deal with, he became much more widely known for his consulting knowledge concerning products and manufacturing operations. Many of these same salespeople later started their own industrial distributorships.

The number of distributorships has increased over the years but there is still a sprinkling of "old timers" around. Twenty percent of our present day companies were actively involved in business before 1900, some were established as early as 1870, and a few before that. One such company is the Moore-Handley Hardware Company, which opened its doors soon after the Civil War. The evolutionary development of the industry can be traced from the John W. Berry Supply Company which was established in 1824. The Berry Company stocked supplies for factories and railroad shops during the industrial revolution.

The distributor in the early 1900s had gas lights, crank telephones if the company was in a metropolitan area, a cuspidor, and a roll-top desk. Inventory consisted of fasteners (such as nuts, bolts and rivets), power transmission equipment (such as leather belts and wooden sheaves) and bundles of rope, hand tools and abrasives.

Fifteen

Turn Of The Century

In the late 1880s and early 1890s, trade associations were in the process of trying to be formed to cope with the competition-crushing "trusts." It was important that trade associations be formed for the mutual protection of their members. The lack of agreement killed the first attempt of building an association in 1891 after only three years. It was revived again in 1894, but still was ahead of its time. All of these early efforts, however, were to bear fruit with the establishment of the Southern Supply and Machinery Dealers Association in April of 1902. They agreed to meet in Charleston, South Carolina and discuss mutual interests and goals.

The morning of April 2, 1902, the meeting was called to order by Mr. C. B. Carter, and, in accordance with the program, an address was delivered by Mr. C. B. Jenkins, of the Cameron-Barkley Company of Charleston, entitled, "Why We Organize." In his address, Mr. Jenkins defined organization as the act or process of arranging and getting in proper working order. He stated that the reasons for the meeting were to organize an association for the promotion of distribution, friendlier communications with competitors and for socialness. More importantly, Mr. Jenkins went on to say that associations must be formed to diminish the ruinous competition of the trusts. In view of these gigantic trusts, Jenkins said, it was time for the distributors to get together and discuss their own positions and the treatment they should receive.

Mr. Carter presented letters received from different firms all over the country, responding to invitations sent them to join the association. Companies such as Young and Heintz and Briggs Machinery & Supply Co. from Dallas, Texas, Mayer and Company, Norfolk, Virginia, and Southern Supply Company, Mobile, Alabama, responded, some regretting that they could not attend or would not be interested in membership and others congratulating the movement.

The By-Laws were adopted, article by article, and by the end of the 16th day of April, 1902, the constitution was ratified and a new slate of executive officers had been secured. The association thus established still exists in great strength and has significant industrial impact.

The members had invited numerous manufacturers to attend the meeting. The manufacturers organized and became the American Supply and Machinery Manufacturers Association in April, 1905. However, in the meantime the industrial distributors in the northern portion of the United States were also forming the National Association. The two distribution associations were known as the Southern and National Industrial Distributor Associations. These two associations merged in 1988 to form the Industrial Distributors Association (IDA).

It seems as though history repeats itself, or never changes, because the topics discussed at the early meetings are some of the same topics discussed today: equitable margins, the manufacturer's resistance to the increase of profit margins, price cutting, the passing on of manufacturer's increased costs causing narrowed profit margins, the ever increasing sales expense and higher costs for the distributor. It also seems as though these problems are as prevalent today as they were in 1904. Some of the abuses which existed in the industry then, as well as today, were taking cash discounts after the period had elapsed, taking special returned goods privileges beyond reasonable measure and price cutting.

In 1908 the electrical jobbers association met for the adoption of their first constitution. In December the Electrical Supply Jobbers Association (which would later become the National Association of Electrical Distributors, NAED) met with 79 charter members in attendance in Niagara Falls, Canada. Their objective was to promote friendly relations among electrical distributors, and standardize and market high grade electrical merchandise.

Soon after the industrial distributor associations were formed they banded together to support the development of a trade publication for their industry called <u>Mill Supplies</u>. One of the objectives of the new magazine was to promote harmony within the industry. This was the theme of the 1911 convention held in Louisville.

Early 1915 found the country in the midst of a depression. However, the United Kingdoms orders for war materials to protect themselves from Germany gave greater stimulus to the American economy through the sales of explosives and iron and steel. Many neutral countries turned to America for manufactured goods since exports from Germany and several European ports had been curtailed. The industry had such a boom that in 1916 it was impossible to buy machine tools for immediate delivery.

The inevitable occurred and the United States entered into a full-scale war with Germany in 1918. Manufacturers and distributors alike who had banded together for mutual protection now banded together and pledged their support to the United States government with no reservations. Their pledge was to be of complete service to our country.

Sales volumes through mill supply houses grew rapidly. One reason for this rapid increase was the governments purchase of 22,000 war planes. An order for 22,000 planes, for example, would demand a purchase of hand tools of approximately $150 per plane.

Price escalations and inflation are always a problem in war times, and World War I was no exception. However, immediately following the end of the war in 1919, prices dropped and production declined as the nation entered a recession. The 1920s business outlook was described at that time as "a very sick patient who is convalescing and who must be careful to avoid a setback."

Industrial and electrical jobbers experienced a period of unrest and tension, and post-war problems increased. By 1921 approximately 20 percent of the industrial, manufacturing and transportation workers were unemployed. Most distributors had to adjust to smaller sales volumes and lower prices. They also experienced some inflation during these times. Orders were hard to come by and getting people to pay their debts even harder.

By 1922, post-war inventories had been reduced and business returned to a fairly normal state. Customers of distributors of iron, steel and coal were back in business. As a whole, the first 25 years of the twentieth century was a period of fairly substantial growth. Much of this meant improved sales for distributors, particularly in the area of highway development. Both road construction and the automobile industry provided sources of revenue. Also, the trucking industry enhanced distributor sales by making transportation much quicker from factory to end user.

The war had demanded increased capacity and improved machinery, which created additional markets for consumable supplies for the distributor. This new technology gave rise to additional new industries such as electric washing machines, electric refrigerators and radio sets. The American home and its occupants were developing costlier tastes and desires. Radio apparatus annual sales climbed into the millions by 1925. The entire range of products was boosted by hundreds which sold through distributors. One humorous result of this burgeoning technical growth was that in 1926, the United States Patent Office closed its doors because they said "everything that can be invented had been invented."

Mass production (a term which was becoming a way of American life by the 1920s) is useless without "mass distribution." However, mass distribution of highly technical products demanded special services which were rendered best by the distributor. This forced the distributor salesperson to increase his technical expertise and also to become accustomed to selling to engineers and persons other than purchasing managers. The average distributor of this era had an inventory of approximately $100,000 worth of industrial and electrical supplies for mining, oil field, shipping, automobile, railway, and metal removal industries as well as for blacksmiths, textile mills and public utilities.

Even though many of the distributors who had been in business for several years were skeptical of those who wished to specialize, many specialty distributors sprang up. One such specialty was machine tools. Machine tool manufacturers felt that the average "dealer" (distributor) could not provide the technical expertise to sell machine tools. Some machine tool manufacturers still hold that concept today, even though broad general line distributors do have specialty teams within their organization who sell and service machine tools.

Having endured World War I and the serious portion of

the depression which followed, the country once again moved into times of prosperity. President Coolidge promised a $300 million tax cut for 1926, while 4 million cars were being manufactured annually. It seemed like the prosperity would never end. However, President Hoover warned that speculation in stocks and bonds was too great.

During this time, the distributor had been particularly affected by the manufacturers selling directly to the consumers and by serious price cutting. Alvin Smith of Smith-Courtney Co., Richmond, VA, one of the early leaders of the Southern Industrial Distributors Association, called it "a year of the most unbridled, ignorant and unscientific price cutting we have ever been through."

Some pessimistic individuals thought that the change to selling direct would kill the small distributor. It did not, but even during the greatest prosperity in the 1920s, the inflationary factor kept distributors from making a healthy profit because of the higher operating costs. The distributors felt that their suppliers (manufacturers) were not true partners in their selling efforts, because the manufacturers would sell direct to the customer when they had an opportunity to do so. Most manufacturers had no proven distributor policies and were not willing to generate them.

This was also an era of specialization, high production and customers who wanted high service levels. The manufacturers felt that the distributors could not perform this service as well as they could.

In 1925, a number of changes occurred in the industry. Membership in the associations was up and a new contributor, The Industrial Distributor and Salesman, the predecessor of the present Industrial Distribution magazine, coupled with Mill Supplies magazine, was to influence change throughout this era. The crux of the message was that the industrial distributors were about to go out of business from lack of identification with the industry unless they could convince customers of the value of the services they provided.

In 1926, the three associations agreed to have the Triple Convention on the cruise ship "Noronic." Aboard the ship, the Mill Supply Council was born. The trip was later called "The Peace Ship." The convention gave rise in the next three years to the development of group responsibility and close harmony which have suffered only minor setbacks since that time. The responsibility of the committee was to outline the distributors function and a clear cut code of ethics and discuss all the pure practices prevalent in the distribution industry. By 1930, the joint merchandising committee was organized to help sell the industry both to itself and its industrial customers. The objective of the committee was to get both suppliers and customers to recognize the importance of the industrial distributor. A slogan, "Distributors service industry economically," was adopted and advertising plans were made.

The emergence of three national companies, General Electric, Westinghouse and Graybar Electric Supply Company, gave renewed hope for prosperity.

The stock market crashed in 1929, however, and business was once again in depression. The problem was compounded because the distributor was getting only 35 percent of all supply purchases from large customers. Strong sales and promotional programs were the only things which helped build faith in the service provided by distributors.

Sixteen

The Great Depression

Electrical wholesalers saw their sales volumes drop off 60 percent between 1929 and 1933. In order to help this faltering situation, the National Electrical Wholesalers Association (NEWA) changed its direction. The first major effort was the development of the "Code of Fair Competition" for the electrical wholesaling industry, which established federal fair trade guidelines.

One positive experience which came out of the depression was the strengthening of the relationship between distributors and manufacturers. It forced manufacturers to close their branch outlets, decrease their sales forces, and begin to rely on the distributors for available sales. With hand-to-mouth buying there was little temptation to buy or sell direct.

President Roosevelt's National Recovery Act (NRA), passed in 1933, had a dual purpose: to help rid business of destructive trade practices through fair competition policies and to increase consumer purchasing power by establishing minimum wages and maximum hours. The act outlawed sales prices below cost or below suggested resale prices, discrimination between buyers and disguised price concessions. The distributors codes, called Blue Eagles, lasted until May, 1935, when the NRA was invalidated by the Supreme Court.

The Supreme Court also knocked out the Code of Fair Competition of the electrical industry. NEWA members quickly substituted a Code of Practices which had already been worked out with the Federal Trade Commission. The demise of the NRA also gave NEWA an opportunity to establish new membership requirements that would ultimately attract those wholesalers who were fully and ethically committed to the industry.

Because of the NRA, distributors were bonded together as never before and local distributor organizations were boosted into dominance. One such organization was the Central States Industrial Distributors Association (now a part of IDA) founded in 1933, with Wendall H. Clark of Samuel Harris & Company from Chicago as its first president.

Another of Roosevelt's New Deal legislative measures was the Wagner Act, passed in 1936, to institutionalize collective bargaining. Also in 1936, the Social Security Act came into being, and in 1937, resale price agreements were enforced by the Miller-Tydings Act. In 1938, the Wage and Hour Law was passed, which has affected American industries ever since. Hiring practices and pay scales were emerging governmental interests.

The years 1936 and 1937 saw electrical wholesalers establishing record-breaking sales volumes. But by the end of 1937, a sharp drop in business was seen. This rapid decline in sales created inventory and collection problems which this industry had not yet experienced. Inventories were overflowing, and credit, fully given in the preceding decade, was being tightened.

By 1939, industry cost studies indicated the distributors total share of the market had dropped substantially from the upsurge the industry had felt in the early twenties. The past decade had brought down some of the old industrial distributor "houses," but strong ones remained the nucleus of the distribution industry.

The decade also had established new governmental agencies with whom electrical and industrial distributors had to learn to work. The New Deal had forced these industries into compliance, building into their already firm structures accommodations for new forms of taxation and regulation, wage and hour laws, social security, etc. In spite of the government intervention, it was an era which saw new and exciting products boost the living standards of the United States to the highest of any in the world.

Seventeen

The War Years

Hitler invaded Poland in 1939. By January, 1940, sales figures began to rise despite the darkened days of the foreign war. Optimism was in the air as distributors increased their inventories in hopes that foreign nations involved in their "own" war would buy from American stock-piles.

In those early days of war — as soon as Americans began to realize that the "foreign" war was in fact our own — distributors proved again and again by performance that they could do the job better and less expensively than anyone else. They were begining to develop an awareness of new demands that they might have to meet in the near future. To distributors, new demands meant buying problems, lengthened deliveries, hiring and training new employees, and space shortages. But distributors were a strongly-knit group by this time and met the demands head on.

In December, 1940, the Office of Production Management, a government agency, took over control of production and raw materials which could be used in the war effort. Distributors and manufacturers were called on to help. However, some agencies of the government were staffed by so-called economics experts with two schools of thought about distributors: the "direct selling" and the "anti-middleman" concepts. Not having done business with the Army, Navy and

Army Air Corp for very long, the wholesaler distributors were completely surprised when they were brought under fire and summoned by these services to explain and defend their business postures. In order to retain their policies and procedures, the industry had to demonstrate conclusively to the satisfaction of the armed services that they were actually saving money by using the distributors. The distributors proved their case.

A National Defense Committee was formed in 1941 by ASMMA, NIDA and SIDA in order to coordinate defense efforts and control regulations. Non-defense customers began to find it tougher to operate as priorities, for war began to take up more of the distributor's stock. When the Japanese attacked Pearl Harbor in December, 1941, distributor's sales volume was $1.8 billion. Inventories and daily orders were 30 percent higher than the previous year, personnel up 20 percent, average order size up from $13.85 to $25, inventory turnover up from 5.4 to 7, and direct shipments down from 11.84 percent to 9 percent. War production was at its peak. Costs were up, but so were profits.

By 1943, the distributor was winning the battle for recognition. The industrial wholesaler's position was also more positive as the war years focused upon the vital part distributors were playing in our country.

As World War II was coming to a close, the 1944 Triple Convention met in Chicago. Post-war problems could be seen on the horizon: e.g., manpower, contract termination, surplus stock disposal, re-evaluation of sales methods, and post-war competition. Robert Black of Black & Decker Manufacturing Company suggested adapting a way to facilitate contracts between distributors and manufacturers in the future. The war had disrupted many manufacturer-distributor relationships and mending had to be done.

The war ended in 1945. The United States dropped the atomic bomb on Hiroshima and Nagasaki, Japan. We celebrated V-E Day (Victory in Europe) and V-J Day (Victory in Japan) that year. The American people were pleased that the war was finally over and were anxious to get back to peace and prosperity.

A new type of wholesale distributor had emerged during the war. Sales and service oriented, management-intensive distributors began to organize their sales efforts, survey their markets, measure performance and concentrate on sales programs and training efforts to gain greater market share.

The industry also had seen new concepts emerge, and coined the phrase "mass distribution" to go with the "mass production" concept. With mass distribution and production being demanded by the American public, better selling techniques had to be developed.

"Better Selling" was the theme of the 1946 distributors convention in Atlantic City. Arch Morris, Publisher of <u>Mill Supplies</u>, wrote about the meeting, "This industry is united as never before for cooperative action in meeting common problems. Having attained this... it is not going to be very difficult to button the loose ends in distributor-manufacturer relationships..."

By 1947, handling costs for distributors were on the rise as the post-war slump receded. The cost to handle an order was up from $5 to $15. However, sales were improving, inventories were larger, and distributors were hiring more salesmen to "get the orders."

The years following the war were in many ways spectacular. Men and women returned from military service and entered educational institutions or started work- study programs on the G. I. Bill of Rights. Years later, this proved to be one of the better expenditures of federal funds because it was not a dole but truly an investment in Americas greatest resource -- its people. Those who came back were also ready to "get back to living." They took husbands and wives and started families right away. This surge of children, known as the "post-war baby boom," affected all facets of the American way of life from the number of public school teachers needed to the supplies required to manufacture automobiles and build new homes.

During the war, domestic goods were almost non-existent. Everyone had been called upon to sacrifice in order to support the war effort. Staple foods like meat and sugar were rationed and almost no domestic automobiles were manufactured between 1941 and 1945. During the same period, employment approached the 100 percent level with almost every available person working. Wages were increasing also. The irony was that masses of the people had money for the first time since the "crash of '29," but could not spend it because virtually all consumer goods were going to the war effort.

Three other factors which influenced the industrial economy following the war were the desire for mobility by young people, the amount of oil available to make gasoline, and idle manufacturing capacity. Young men and women had come out of the mountains of Tennessee and from the plains of Kansas and had been shipped to Europe, North Africa or the South Pacific. When they came back to the States they were not satisfied to go home and stay there. They wanted to go to New York and to California, but they needed and wanted their own automobiles. Factories which had been changed earlier to make trucks and tanks for war were reconverted to make cars and pickups once again.

During the war, America searched for and found oil to field a mobile army. Oil production neared three million barrels a day by 1947, but domestic consumption was only half of the potential production. The desire to go and see, coupled with the availability of gasoline, the productive capabilities of manufacturers to make automobiles, and people with buying power, turned America into an automobile-based economy.

Television was introduced in 1947. In addition, consumers were demanding more major household appliances than ever before. The heavy post-war electrification of rural areas brought the cities into the country and much of rural America into the cities.

The 1948 distributors convention achieved a milestone in manufacturer-distributor relationships with the inauguration of the "contact booth" program originally suggested in 1944 by Robert Black of Black & Decker Manufacturing Company. Some 200 manufacturers contracted for booths manned with executives. The purpose of the booths was to place corporate executives (decision makers) strategically in a central location so that it was easy to make direct contact to get immediate answers to pressing problems.

A slackening of industrial activity was seen in 1949 across the country, but industry began to bounce back by 1950 with the threat of a new war, later to be called the Korean Conflict. With the threat of another war, and the government beginning to rebuild military priorities, "stockpiling", "allocating" and "critical shortages" again became familiar words to distributors.

Since 1950

The war years set the stage for an ever-increasing demand for the services of wholesale distributors. Convincing buyers that the cost to purchase goods is actually less when bought through distributors rather than direct from the manufacturer is still a constant problem for distributors, but is being accomplished by providing customers with data which substantiate the facts.

In recent years, an ever-increasing number of well-educated purchasing managers are determining to purchase from distributors. As the move is made to the quality process, not only will they buy from distributors instead of direct from manufacturers, but they will buy from fewer and better qualified distributors. This makes the distribution industry an exciting and challenging career field because it is one of the few uncharted frontiers of business left in America where young people can make a place for themselves early in their careers and continue to advance all of their working lives.